Praying
LIKE
JESUS

Praying LIKE JESUS

Discovering The Pattern of Godly Prayer

Julie-Allyson Ieron

MOODY PRESS
CHICAGO

All Scripture quotations, unless otherwise indicated, are taken from the *Holy Bible, New International Version*®. NIV®. Copyright © 1973, 1978, 1984 by International Bible Society. Used by permission of Zondervan Publishing House. All rights reserved.

Scripture quotations marked NKJV are taken from the *New King James Version.* Copyright © 1982 by Thomas Nelson, Inc. Used by permission. All rights reserved.

Scripture quotations marked KJV are taken from the King James Version.

Scripture quotations marked NASB are taken from the *New American Standard Bible*®, © Copyright The Lockman Foundation 1960, 1962, 1963, 1968, 1971, 1972, 1973, 1975, 1977, 1995. Used by permission.

Scripture quotations marked TLB are taken from *The Living Bible* copyright © 1971. Used by permission of Tyndale House Publishers, Inc., Wheaton, Illinois 60189. All rights reserved.

Scripture quotations marked NLT are taken from the *Holy Bible, New Living Translation,* copyright © 1996. Used by permission of Tyndale House Publishers, Inc., Wheaton Illinois 60189, U.S.A. All rights reserved.

Scripture quotations marked *The Message* are from *The Message,* copyright © by Eugene H. Peterson 1993, 1994, 1995. Used by permission of NavPress Publishing Group.

Library of Congress Cataloging-in-Publication Data

Ieron, Julie-Allyson.
    Praying like Jesus : discovering the pattern of godly prayer / Julie-Allyson Ieron.
    p. cm.
    Includes bibliographical references.
    ISBN 0-8024-8337-2
    1. Jesus Christ--Prayers. 2. Bible. N. T. John XVII--Criticism, interpretation, etc. 3. Prayer--Christianity. I. Title.

BV234 .I34 2001
248.3´2--dc21   00-051127

1 3 5 7 9 10 8 6 4 2

Printed in the United States of America

I lovingly dedicate this book to my grandparents

Helen & Tony
Cherubina & Nick,

whose godliness and praying hearts
I consider my richest treasure and most valued heritage

CONTENTS

Part Five
God's Promises to Us

Part Six
Interests Beyond Ourselves

Part Seven
Postlude to Prayer

ACKNOWLEDGMENTS

I want to express my appreciation to so many people who played key roles in the preparation of this book. First and foremost, I want to thank the prayer warriors who encouraged me and prayed me through the writing process—especially John and Joyce (my parents), Helen Scarlatta (my grandmother), Karen Koch, Beverly Dalesandro, Nancy Hudson and her Bible study group, Ruth French and her prayer line, and countless others.

To the Moody Press team: Thank you for catching the vision of this book and for inviting me to write it. To Bill Thrasher, who sponsored the book; Elsa Mazon, who acquired it; Cheryl Dunlop, who patiently and meticulously edited it; Carolyn McDaniel, who worked tirelessly in typesetting; Joe and Mary Ragont, who designed the cover; and to the marketing and sales team who will see that this book reaches your hands—my deepest appreciation.

Our prayer is that our Lord will use this book to reveal to you many truths about Himself, that our efforts will bring eternal fruit, and, most important, that God will receive all the glory.

Many blessings to you.

JESUS' HIGH PRIESTLY PRAYER (JOHN 17)

¹After Jesus said this, he looked toward heaven and prayed: "Father, the time has come. Glorify your Son, that your Son may glorify you. ²For you granted him authority over all people that he might give eternal life to all those you have given him. ³Now this is eternal life: that they may know you, the only true God, and Jesus Christ, whom you have sent. ⁴I have brought you glory on earth by completing the work you gave me to do. ⁵And now, Father, glorify me in your presence with the glory I had with you before the world began.

⁶"I have revealed you to those whom you gave me out of the world. They were yours; you gave them to me and they have obeyed your word. ⁷Now they know that everything you have given me comes from you. ⁸For I gave them the words you gave me and they accepted them. They knew with certainty that I came from you, and they believed that you sent me. ⁹I pray for them. I am not praying for the world, but for those you have given me, for they are yours. ¹⁰All I have is yours, and all you have is mine. And glory has come to me through them. ¹¹I will remain in the world no longer, but they are still in the world, and I am coming to you. Holy Father, protect them by the power of your name—the name you gave me—so that they may be one as we are one. ¹²While I was with them, I protected them and kept them safe by that name you gave me. None has been lost except the one doomed to destruction so that Scripture would be fulfilled.

¹³"I am coming to you now, but I say these things while I am still in the world, so that they may have the full measure of my joy within them. ¹⁴I have given them your word and the world has hated them, for they are not of the world any more than I am of the world. ¹⁵My prayer is not that you take them out of the world but that you protect them from the evil one. ¹⁶They are not of the world, even as I am not of it. ¹⁷Sanctify them by the truth; your word is truth. ¹⁸As you sent me into the world, I have sent them into the world. ¹⁹For them I sanctify myself, that they too may be truly sanctified.

²⁰"My prayer is not for them alone. I pray also for those who will believe in me through their message, ²¹that all of them may be one, Father, just as you are in me and I am in you. May they also be in us so that the world may believe that you have sent me. ²²I have given them the glory that you gave me, that they may be one as we are one: ²³I in them and you in me. May they be brought to complete unity to let the world know that you sent me and have loved them even as you have loved me.

²⁴"Father, I want those you have given me to be with me where I am, and to see my glory, the glory you have given me because you loved me before the creation of the world.

²⁵"Righteous Father, though the world does not know you, I know you, and they know that you have sent me. ²⁶I have made you known to them, and will continue to make you known in order that the love you have for me may be in them and that I myself may be in them."

CHAPTER 1

∞

INTRODUCTION: WHEN GOD PRAYED

∞

I keep asking that the God of our Lord Jesus Christ, the glorious
Father, may give you the Spirit of wisdom and revelation, so that you
may know him better. I pray also that the eyes of your heart may be
enlightened in order that you may know the hope to which he has
called you, the riches of his glorious inheritance in the saints, and his
incomparably great power for us who believe.

—EPHESIANS 1:17–19a

In most prayer meetings we make time for individuals to call out prayer requests. We collectively list off the needs of all who are ill and ask for something we call "traveling mercies" for those away on vacation. But have you ever attempted to give a request for something as nebulous as spiritual growth, your journey toward godliness, or a deeper understanding of God's presence?

I have. And most often those requests are met with blank stares.

Amid the recitation of illnesses and financial needs, these seem out of place, easily brushed aside and quickly forgotten. They are intangible, impractical by comparison to more immediate needs.

It seems to me that the people who *are* talking about deepening relationships with God and empowering the prayer life are the elite few who regularly embark on long-term spiritual pilgrimages and enjoy weeks of wordless contemplation during silent retreats in the wildernesses of God's creation.

But what of the rest of us—ordinary folk for whom a mere hour of silent contemplation is a luxury found only in the netherworld? Can we not go deeper in our communication with God? Or are we forever to drive up to the order window of heaven asking for a half order of God to go, please, and make it snappy?

A thousand times, no! Going deeper with God on a daily basis is not only possible, but eminently practical. That's what this book is all about. We'll be like code-breakers, intercepting communication (recorded by the apostle John) that overhears God the Son (Jesus) talking with God the Father. Our mission: to break the code and learn His prayer secrets.

We'll make our examination in small daily discoveries and will begin to apply these new principles to real prayer—in real life— right away.

Why are we beginning with Jesus' prayer from John 17 instead of the more traditional starting point of the Lord's Prayer? That earlier prayer (found in Matthew 6 and Luke 11) has become so familiar to many of us that we can gloss right over the truths it contains. Because we've memorized it, chanted it, and sung it for what seems eons, we feel we've mastered it, graduated from Prayer 101 as it were, and moved on. But when Jesus allowed His followers to overhear His conversation with the Father immediately before His trip to the cross, He offered us a meaty perspective on the depth of relationship that prayer can offer between God and His children.

Additionally, because of its proximity to His trip to the cross, the prayer in John 17 reveals what was weighing most heavily on Jesus' mind at the world's most crucial moment. Jesus' words to His Father are intimate and passionate. In being privy to that communication, can we not learn more about communicating with the mind of our mysterious God?

What *does* God say to God?

That question has always fascinated me. So much so that when I looked for a Scripture to carry in my day planner every day during 1999, I prayerfully selected John 17, the passage that translators label "The High Priestly Prayer."

All year I read and reread that passage. I contemplated. I studied. I mused. Finally in desperation some time during November, I prayed. (You're thinking, *Duh, what took you so long?*) Only then did it begin to come alive. I began to breathe in a fresh breath—then gulp after gulp—of the fresh air of His love. And I caught a new vision into those areas of my communication with Him that He wants me to improve.

So, my first prayer in this area of my own spiritual need for growth was actually a request for insight. As the apostle Paul would put it, I prayed "that the eyes of [my] heart [would] be enlightened" (Ephesians 1:18).

Let's begin this study together with a similar prayer.

Note that the suggested prayers in this collection are fragments. Some adapt the words of Scripture, while others are based on the works of classical writers and lyricists. Be assured, the prayers are fragmented intentionally. We'll start on one track together and leave openings to enable all of us to create our own private and intimate communication with God—*our* Father.

Rather than proceeding verse by verse through the prayer, I have grouped chapters into topical sections. Some verses we will revisit in several chapters, examining their various nuances and purposes. We will begin by focusing on those prayers that are of greatest importance to God our Father.

Now then: Let us pray.

PERSONAL PRAYER STARTER

My Father in heaven,
*   I have told others that I know You, but I realize my knowledge of You is disappointingly limited. I have only made time to see a small portion of Your character; I have discerned so little about who You really are. So, with the apostle Paul, I ask now, as I study Your Son's prayer in the days ahead, that You will give me the spirit of wisdom and revelation that I may know You better.*
*   Enlighten the eyes of my heart, so that I may see You as . . .*
*   Enlighten me also to Your hand at work in . . .*
*   Allow me to know the plans You have established in the area of . . .*
*   I thank You for Your willingness to be known.*

PART ONE

Prelude to PRAYER

*If we can come to understand what God
the Son said to God the Father on our
behalf, perhaps we can enhance our own
communication with our Creator,
our Master, our heavenly Friend.*

CHAPTER 2

❧

PRAYER'S PREREQUISITE

❧

The most important Person who ever existed loves you and me!
The Creator of the universe has revealed Himself as having
the tender heart of a loving Father, and has by His Spirit made us
His true-born children. He knows your name, He knows my name,
He laughs and weeps with us. In Him we have discovered that
we are valued infinitely far above our worth.

—GRAHAM KENDRICK[1]

*O*ne of my favorite authors is the nineteenth-century visionary Jules Verne. In fact, as I write I am sitting in a hotel room in Paris with a volume of Verne's *Journey to the Center of the Earth* at my bedside.

As Verne's classic story opens, Professor Lidenbrock and his nephew Axel decode an ancient cryptic message that urges them to undertake a perilous journey into the deepest recesses of the Earth, to places of great mystery where their eyes will take in marvelous scenes that, though they have existed for eons, have been largely impenetrable to dwellers on *terra firma*.

Like the fictitious professor and his nephew, we too are decoding a message that invites us on a journey. Will it be fraught with peril? Perhaps. But then what would life be without a little danger? Certainly, our trip will be rewarding as we delve deep into the unknown (but knowable) world of prayer. Where Verne's explorers encountered monstrous creatures of the deep, we instead will have the unparalleled opportunity to encounter the face and the heart of God.

Even as Verne's explorers had to take several days to assemble and pack the essentials before embarking on their journey, so too we must make our own preparations before we can embark on ours. Our most pivotal preparation is to be certain each of us has a thorough understanding of the first word Jesus intoned in His high priestly prayer: *Father.* Not the corporate *Our Father* of the Lord's Prayer. Just *Father.* Implied here is an intimate, personal relationship, one that each of us must initiate before we can expect our prayers to reach their intended target.

Several years ago I read an interview of a Hollywood star whose acting work I respect. The interviewer, trying to get past the barrage of usual questions, asked her what she does when she is in an overwhelmingly frustrating situation. Her answer rings all too true: "I try to pray," she said. Not "I pray," just "I try to." Leaving open the question of whether or not she gets through to heaven.

I don't know whether this actress has a personal relationship with God. But I can't help but wonder how many of us know we ought to communicate with God, we may even try to do it, yet we haven't made the proper preparations for the journey—we haven't established a relationship with Him. It is, after all, rather audacious for one who doesn't know God personally to reach a crisis and suddenly try to storm the doors of heaven with requests or demands. As strangers to Him, what right have we to make requests of Him? How can we even expect admittance into His throne room? We can try to pray, but like this actress we will continue to be left wondering whether our prayers *might* get through.

I submit to you that the code to unlock the access portal of heaven is the simple address that Jesus used when beginning His prayer. *Father.* Not only does He claim God as His Father, but He invites us to do the same. "When you pray," He told His followers, "go into your room, close the door and pray to *your* Father, who is unseen" (Matthew 6:6a, italics added). Even I—a flawed, puny human from the heavenly perspective—can call God *Father,* if He has adopted me into His family.

This adoption is free on our side, but it came at great cost to God the Father and His Son Jesus. In his letter to the believers in Ephesus, the apostle Paul explained,

> Long ago, even before he made the world, God loved us and chose us in Christ to be holy and without fault in his eyes. His unchanging plan has always been to adopt us into his own family by bringing us to himself through Jesus Christ. And this gave him great pleasure. . . . He is so rich in kindness that he purchased our freedom through the blood of his Son, and our sins are forgiven. (Ephesians 1:4–5, 7 NLT)

Why did the purchase of our freedom require the shedding of Jesus' blood? Well, no matter how good we may think we have been, the Bible tells us that every one of us has sinned—has fallen short of God's holy standard of utter perfection (Romans 3:23). It matters not whether our sin is small or great in our own eyes; even one little transgression of His law is enough to disqualify us from access into God's presence and from our adoption into His family. And the Bible tells us sin must be paid for with blood, with death.

As we continue our study on prayer, we will delve deeper into this concept of God's perfection, which we call holiness, but for now it is enough to acknowledge that on our own there is nothing we can do to hold to this standard.

Yet there was something God could do. He initiated a way—the only possible way—for us to be made spotless in His sight. But this required that someone without blemish or sin give up His life in our place. That someone was His only Son, Jesus, who laid down His own human life two thousand years ago, letting His lifeblood splatter down from a cross and puddle in the dust of a hill outside Jerusalem, taking the penalty for my sins and yours upon His perfectly sinless shoulders.

Jesus agonized over the burden of our sin, over all our pain, and especially over our distance from the God who loves us. He did this so we could be established with all the rights and privileges as sons and daughters of God. He bore our guilt, and now we can be free of it. And the amazing part is that all the pain was on His side; He made it so easy for us to be clean that it sometimes seems to our constricted minds that we must do something more to become worthy.

Yet all we need do is follow Jesus' prescription: "Whoever hears my word and believes him who sent me has eternal life and will not be condemned; he has crossed over from death to life" (John 5:24). Or in the words the apostle Paul wrote to the Romans, "For if you confess with your mouth that Jesus is Lord and believe in your heart that God raised him from the dead, you will be saved. For it is by believing in your heart that you are made right with God, and it is by confessing with your mouth that you are saved" (Romans 10:9–10 NLT).

So, I invite you right now to pray the following prayer along with me. It is a prayer that will help you confess with your mouth that Jesus is Lord, as a confirmation of what you have come to believe in your heart. Perhaps you've prayed a prayer like this before; perhaps this will be your first time. Even if it is your first time, I assure you that God will hear and answer, and from the moment you speak it, He will call you His own child. Just like a prince or princess in a king's court, you will now be welcome to have an audience before the King of the universe at any time, for any reason, without appointment and without uncertainty.

The thirteenth-century Italian author Dante Alighieri wrote his first masterpiece of poetry when he was a young person, as a tribute to the woman he loved. He called it *La Vita Nuova*. Its opening, loosely translated, offers this powerful statement about the day he met the love of his life: "In that book which is my memory . . . I find one chapter that says, 'Here begins a new life.'"

And so, if you are praying this prayer for the first time, or if you are praying it again as a recommitment to building a vibrant relationship with God through Jesus Christ, then we can say along with Dante, "Here begins *la vita nuova*."

PERSONAL PRAYER STARTER

Almighty God,
I come before You in Jesus' name — not because of any merit of my own, but only because Jesus, Your Son, makes it possible.
Never before have I felt more aware of my sinfulness. I confess to You that I have sinned by . . .
Although I could never earn my way into Your good stead, even so, You sacrificed Your Son to give me the opportunity to become Your child.
I reach out to accept the free gift of forgiveness You offer me. Please apply Christ's blood to my account, forgive my sin, and make me clean before You.
Now I turn my life over to Your control. My desire is to build a relationship with You and to . . .
I am grateful to You for this new life and for . . .

NOTE

1. Graham Kendrick, *Worship* (Kingsway Publications, 1984), 78.

CHAPTER 3

SNAPSHOTS
OF GOD

O worship the King, all-glorious above,
And gratefully sing His pow'r and His love;
Our Shield and Defender, the Ancient of Days,
Pavilioned in splendor, and girded with praise.
—ROBERT GRANT (1779–1838), "O WORSHIP THE KING."

*M*odern writer Eugene Peterson made the profound statement that prayer is not something we human beings initiate; it is something the Creator initiates. "Prayer is not something we think up to get God's attention or enlist His favor. Prayer is *answering* speech. The first word is God's word."[1] Theologian J. I. Packer takes that concept a step further: "Were we left to ourselves, any praying we did would both start and end with ourselves, for our natural self-centeredness knows no bounds. . . . But Jesus' pattern prayer . . . tells us to start with God: for lesson one is to grasp that God matters infinitely more than we do."[2]

If that is true, then when we respond with our prayers, it might be helpful to understand something about the character of the Initiator, the Father of the First Word (John 1:1).

When we pray to our Father in heaven, exactly whom are we addressing? Scripture gives us many clues, or partial pictures of

God. Although none of them is sufficient to describe Him thoroughly (as He is beyond anything our finite language could describe), a few phrases can illuminate our minds for starters. One phrase Bible writers use in both 1 Samuel 15:29 and Hebrews 9:5 is "The Glory."

Intriguing. But what is glory?

The *American Heritage Dictionary* defines it as "majestic beauty and splendor; resplendence." Even in this definition we encounter words that are beyond our everyday vocabulary, words we may have heard or even used, yet whose depth of meaning we probably have never plumbed. Those who worship in more contemporary settings may often sing the popular chorus "Majesty" that Jack Hayford wrote as a response to a biblical view of God's glory. Yet do we understand what it means for us to worship God's majesty?

Outside the confines of our church services, outside our cloistered cliques where we speak *Christianese,* when do we use the word *glory?* Not very often, I'm afraid. And not to the fullness of its meaning. We describe the first sunny, warm Saturday of spring as a "glorious" day. What we really mean is it is a perfectly beautiful day. That doesn't even begin to do the word justice—at least in comparison to what we mean when we refer to God's glory.

Here's how three Bible men, from three different generations, describe God's glory. The prophet Isaiah sets the stage. "The year King Uzziah died I saw the Lord! He was sitting on a lofty throne, and the Temple was filled with his glory" (Isaiah 6:1 TLB). Isaiah saw a glory that was voluminous. A glory that filled and overflowed an entire temple. A glory that caused him to fall on his face in unabashed humility.

The apostle John sheds more light as he describes his first glimpse of the glorified Christ in heaven: "His head and hair were white like wool, as white as snow, and his eyes were like blazing fire. His feet were like bronze glowing in a furnace, and his voice was like the sound of rushing waters. In his right hand he held seven stars, and out of his mouth came a sharp double-edged sword. His face was like the sun shining in all its brilliance" (Revelation 1:14–16).

Note that the apostle John had walked side-by-side with Jesus on this earth, had laid his head on the Master's shoulder, had even seen the Lord's luminescent countenance on the Mount of Transfiguration. And yet he knelt in awe of the One he saw standing before him whose eyes blazed like fire.

The prophet Ezekiel adds color to the picture: "Above the expanse over their heads was what looked like a throne of sapphire, and high above on the throne was a figure like that of a man. I saw that from what appeared to be his waist up he looked like glowing metal, as if full of fire, and that from there down he looked like fire; and brilliant light surrounded him. Like the appearance of a rainbow in the clouds on a rainy day, so was the radiance around him. This was the appearance of the likeness of the glory of the Lord" (Ezekiel 1:26–28).

Later in the book of Revelation the apostle John adds, "And the one who sat there had the appearance of jasper and carnelian. A rainbow, resembling an emerald, encircled the throne" (Revelation 4:3).

The descriptions these men use are so out of the everyday that we can scarcely comprehend them. John describes God using the analogy of jasper and carnelian, precious stones, likely red and green. What we know of these are from glimpses of imperfect jewels that sparkle as they reflect the light. They form prisms of color. They are hard, solid, translucent or opaque.

Yet we know enough about God to comprehend that He doesn't just reflect light; He *is* Light. From the core of His being, He is pure, unadulterated, unflickering Light. He is the very source of light. Both John and Ezekiel describe a rainbow that surrounds God's throne. No wonder. He is encircled with the spectrum—a reflection of the unrelenting light that emits from His being.

Rainbows and emeralds. These I understand. But John describes God's glory as a rainbow like an emerald. This is not a picture I can fathom. An emerald rainbow just doesn't fit into the minuscule envelope of my experience. But then again, neither does the Almighty God. He defies human comprehension.

These visions are but a taste of the indescribable glory of God. They are filtered through the frustrating limitations of human description and human vocabulary. Certainly, none of these fortunate few who saw God's glory could fully explain what he was seeing, because there is nothing and no one to whom God can be likened. There is none sufficient that we can say, "Picture this, and you will picture God." Nevertheless, these glimpses give enough insight into His glory to keep us worshiping Him in our prayers for the rest of our lives and even into eternity.

PERSONAL PRAYER STARTER

Glorious One in heaven,

You are so much more, so much greater, so far beyond anything a tiny human mind could begin to imagine. These descriptions of You have helped me understand that You are . . .

Your beauty is matchless, absolutely beyond description. You alone are worthy of the glory that encircles You like a complete rainbow.

All I can do, all I can offer to You is worship from my awestruck, quaking heart, my heart that is . . .

NOTES

1. Eugene Peterson, *Working the Angles: The Shape of Pastoral Integrity* (Grand Rapids: Eerdmans, 1987), 32.

2. J. I. Packer, *I Want to Be a Christian* (Wheaton, Ill.: Tyndale, 1977), 189.

CHAPTER 4

A MATTER
OF LOYALTY

Govern everything by Your wisdom,
O Lord, so that my soul may always be serving You
in the way You will and not as I choose. Let me die to myself
so that I may serve You; let me live to You who are life itself.
—TERESA OF AVILA[1]

I pledge allegiance to the flag . . ." Throughout my childhood, every school day started with this rote statement of loyalty to the United States of America, which included my verbal assent to the preservation of the freedoms upon which my native land was founded. But I'm quite sure the concept of allegiance had little if any impact on me as a child. I didn't feel a duty to the country, nor a responsibility to do anything more taxing (or less self-serving) than finishing my homework, taming my tongue (to avoid punishment), respecting adults (because they said so), and playing with toys and friends every opportunity I got.

As I grew, though, and began to comprehend the truism that with liberty comes responsibility, my pledge of allegiance took on a depth of meaning—or perhaps I should say it took on its first real meaning to me. My loyalty vision sharpened into clear focus when I visited parts of the world where the freedoms I took for granted didn't exist for the common person, and I grew more eager to pledge allegiance to a country that values "liberty and justice for all."

As a college student I visited World War II sites in Europe and war memorials in Washington D.C.; and so I came to appreciate the sacrifice, the complete abandonment of rights thousands of servicemen and women undertook so that I might have these freedoms today. They were so committed to the concept of liberty that they laid down their lives, sacrificed their freedoms, didn't consider their own rights something to be held tightly; in short they relinquished their claim to everything that mattered to them as individuals, all for the sake of the greater good—*my* greater good.

Similarly, now that you and I have established a relationship with God through Jesus Christ—a relationship that offers us freedom from slavery to sin and all its destructive by-products—we ought to initiate our own daily pledge of allegiance to our new country and our new Sovereign Ruler.

Jesus issued the challenge to us, by His example. Philippians 2:5–8 tells us that He did not consider equality with God something to be grasped—something to be held with a death-grip—but instead He laid aside His rights, becoming abandoned to the cause of my salvation to the point of laying down His own life (John 10:18). In beginning his description of all our Lord laid aside for us, the apostle Paul instructs us to pay special attention because we are expected to "have this attitude in yourselves which was also in Christ Jesus" (Philippians 2:5 NASB).

Abandoning my rights leaves a bitter taste in my mouth, as a twenty-first-century Westerner. And yet, when it comes to abandoning myself to God, when I move past my initial knee-jerk emotions, what do I really have to lose? I am abandoning my will to the One whose will is far superior to mine.

As I consider this prerequisite, this building block of a vibrant prayer life of communicating with my Father in heaven, I look to the example of those believers who have gone before me. Consider King David, poet extraordinaire. In the sixteenth Psalm, he chronicled a conversation with God that includes the following statement of faith: "Lord, you alone are my inheritance, my cup of blessing. You guard all that is mine. The land you have given me is a pleasant land. What a wonderful inheritance!" (Psalm 16:5–6 NLT).

According to Lawrence O. Richards, writing in *The Bible Readers Companion,* Psalm 16 shows irrefutable evidence of David's "complete personal commitment to the Lord" resulting in an assurance that "God is in control of David's life and guides his steps. This assurance brings David a matchless sense of security and joy." Richards clarifies this further when he writes, "David affirms that God has sovereignly assigned him his place in life and finds satisfaction in this gift."[2]

So, for David, abandoning himself (or entrusting himself unequivocally) into God's care was anything but a frightening experience. On the contrary, it was a liberating source of joy and comfort.

This is consistent with the full definition of the word *abandon.* According to the *American Heritage Dictionary,* one of the aspects of this rich word, when it is used as a noun, is that of "unbounded enthusiasm" or "exuberance." That's a far cry from a woe-is-me brand of self-sacrifice. Yet I think it is in harmony with the experience of countless Bible characters, David included.

How does all this apply to our lessons on prayer? Oh, we can issue our "gimme lists" to Him in prayer without entrusting ourselves with abandon into His care, and we may even see some limited answers to our prayers. And yet, the depth of communication for which our hearts yearn will never be achieved without the loyalty of our total pledged allegiance.

The beauty of all this is that the by-product of entrusting ourselves to the heavenly Father who loves us is nothing akin to the base subservience we expect to find. Instead, this life overflows with the exuberance—the unbounded joy—that God offers to His committed children. I'm not talking about an artificial happy-all-the-time, I-love-Jesus-now-life-is-easy feeling. But an abiding contentment comes from the assurance that the One who loves me most thoroughly is in charge of my life. That's trust. That's hope. That's living life with abandon to the love of my heavenly Father.

PERSONAL PRAYER STARTER

Father God,
    I must confess, this lesson in prayer is difficult. I like to feel as though I'm in control. So it goes against the grain of my nature to abandon myself to anyone, much less to One I cannot see with my physical eyes.

    And yet, this is what You require, for my own good. With this knowledge, I choose to relinquish my rights to self-determination and abandon myself into Your loving care.

    In particular I abandon to You my rights to . . .

    Daily, I will pledge my allegiance to You and the kingdom of Your Son Jesus by . . .

    Now I thank You for the joy and the assurance that will follow this choice I have made to serve You with my whole self each moment and each day.

NOTES

1. Teresa of Avila (1515–82), Quoted by Chip Stam in Worship Quote of the Week: http://www.wqotw.org/WQOTW/1999_WQs/WQ061599.txt.

2. Lawrence O. Richards, "Psalm 16: The Joy of Fellowship with God," *The Bible Readers Companion,* electronic ed.

CHAPTER 5

YIELDING: A MATTER OF REVERENCE

Take my will, and make it Thine;
It shall be no longer mine.
Take my heart, it is Thine own;
It shall be Thy royal throne.
—FRANCES HAVERGAL, "TAKE MY LIFE AND LET IT BE"

*B*efore we pursue, in earnest, our desire to learn from Jesus' model of prayer, there is yet one more lesson we must observe from His life's example. That lesson is how to yield, how to submit freely and cheerfully, to the authority of our Father in heaven.

If I find it distasteful to abandon myself—to throw myself wholly on His mercy—I am tempted to find it downright noxious to submit my will to anyone or anything, even to God Himself.

When I was in college, one of my pastors explained to me that whenever I am in a difficult situation, I have a couple of coping options. First, I can run away from the problem. This isn't always a bad choice, he explained, but it is not necessarily desirable as the regular pattern of a mature adult. Second, I can stay in the situation with my dukes up: fighting my way through it, protecting my own turf, and punching my way through obstacles. Again, this *can* be a good option, although it also can exacerbate an already strained situation. Those are the obvious choices. When I feel that neither is viable, I tend to feel trapped at an impasse.

Then my pastor explained that I have a third option. He painted the picture of a swimmer who is caught in a strong current. If the swimmer panics and flails his limbs, he is sure to drown. If he tries to paddle against the current, he will make little progress against a power stronger than he. He will end up exhausted yet having made little progress. However, if he determines to allow the current to carry him along, if he lies back and floats with it, he is more likely to be carried to the safety of a calm sea before long.

That third option, making a choice to lie back and float with the flow, is often the best choice in a situation. And it is just that. A choice. My choice. It's not something I'm required to do; instead it is something *I* deem the most viable option.

That advice was life-changing to me. I began to realize that voluntarily submitting to someone outside myself is sometimes the best choice. It's rather like coming up to a four-way intersection that has no stop sign. If two cars approach at the same instant, one driver must make the choice to yield to the other to avoid an accident.

Several instances in Jesus' life illustrate this principle.

One that comes to mind immediately is His pre-ministry years, those years when the Gospel writer tells us that He was subject to Mary and Joseph, His earthly mother and stepfather, and that during that time He increased "in favor with God and men" (Luke 2:52 NKJV).

About this season of Jesus' life, classic author Alfred Edersheim writes, "Generally, this period may be described as that of His true and full Human Development—physical, intellectual, spiritual—of outward submission to man, and inward submission to God, with the attendant results of 'wisdom,' 'favour,' and 'grace.'" Edersheim continues that this time was not wasted in light of Jesus' work as Savior. In fact, he points out, the humiliation of willing submission was the beginning of the process of our salvation.[1]

So, one of the countless sacrifices Jesus made for our salvation was that He placed someone else's interests ahead of His own, voluntarily, intentionally, willingly. Later in the Master's earthly life,

He chose once again to yield or submit to the script His Father had written for His life. The apostle John quotes Jesus as saying, shortly before His final trip to Jerusalem, "No one can kill me without my consent—I lay down my life voluntarily" (John 10:18 TLB).

We can see from Jesus' example that in God's economy, there is a dichotomy in surrendering to His will. In the world as we know it, surrender is equated with admitting defeat. Ultimately, however, surrendering to God's plan for us leads us not to defeat, but to the only way for us to share in His victory.

In our pursuit of the deeper relationship with God through prayer, this is a principle we cannot fail to learn (not that we won't be called to relearn it at various stages of life). If the Son of God laid down His life in submission to the Father's will, how much more must we—as we come into His presence placing before His throne the concerns and circumstances of our lives—how much more must we voice our requests couched in the phrase Jesus used in the Garden of Gethsemane, "Not my will, but yours be done" (Luke 22:42)?

PERSONAL PRAYER STARTER

My Lord, my God,

I feel convicted as I see the example of Your Son so willingly submitting to the agony of the cross simply because it was Your will that He do so.

I have fought against submitting myself to earthly authority—even to Your authority—because I am . . .

Now, I ask You to forgive me for that sin. Make me willing to submit wholly to Your will.

I bring before You the requests on my heart today . . . Now that I have voiced these requests, I say with my Master, "Not my will, but Yours be done."

NOTE

1. Alfred Edersheim, *The Life and Times of Jesus the Messiah*, electronic ed., 2.9.2.

PART TWO

God's INTERESTS

*Before we can begin to consider
making requests for ourselves of God
our Father, we must learn to adore Him
simply because of His holiness,
His majesty, His authority.*

CHAPTER 6

FORGETTING OURSELVES AND FOCUSING ON HIM

"To him who sits on the throne and to the Lamb
be praise and honor and glory and power, for ever and ever!" . . .
And the elders fell down and worshiped.

—REVELATION 5:13–14

$\mathcal{I}$ dislike party games. At parties or bridal showers, I cringe as the hostess brings out a game that is supposed to "break the ice." Too often, "break the ice" translates to "embarrass the guests." But I've never forgotten one party game played years ago in the home of a widow friend of my parents. The hostess counted out fifteen pennies for each guest and placed them in front of the water goblets. Throughout the dinner, anytime a guest was heard to say the word "I," he lost a penny. The one with the most pennies at the end of the meal won.

Before that evening, I'd never taken the time to consider just how often "I" pops up in conversation. Most of my thoughts revolve around myself. And I am the one I talk about most frequently. What a challenge it was to talk about something other than myself and to start listening more to what others were saying.

After the pennies were returned, my mind kept going back to that game. I began measuring the words that come out of my mouth and working to keep the focus of my conversation off "I."

Nowhere is this a more valuable lesson than in our conversation with God. How often have we sung the classic hymn "Holy, Holy, Holy" in corporate worship. Think over any lyrics you can recall from that hymn. Notice there is no use of the words "I" or "me." The focus is not on how great God is because of what He has done *for me*. Instead, the focus of that hymn—and the proper focus of my adoration offering to God—is on *who He is*.

What He has done is great—and we will address our proper response to His gracious work later. But here, our attention in worship and adoration is on His character—His worthiness. The frame is cropped closely around His presence. Nothing else, no one else matters. Only Him. I'm not even in the picture.

At the outset of His prayer, Jesus was concerned that God be glorified, that He be acknowledged for His glory and majesty. Listen to these words: "Glorify your Son, that your Son may glorify you" (John 17:1).

In *An Autobiography of Prayer*, Albert Day writes:

> We never really adore Him, until we arrive at the moment when we worship Him for what He is in Himself, apart from any consideration of the impact of His Divine Selfhood upon our desires and our welfare. Then we love Him for Himself alone. Then we adore Him, regardless of whether any personal benefit is in anticipation or not.[1]

I am only important in that I am the vessel attributing greatness to Him. Prayer of worship is not about me—it is about the Creator, who is exalted far above the earth and the heavens.

PERSONAL PRAYER STARTER

Holy Lord on heaven's throne,
   May You always receive the praise and honor and glory and
power that Your greatness warrants. You and all Your ways are great
and awesome.
   With the angels in heaven, I worship You because You are . . .
   May I bring to You glory in . . .
   Only You deserve all the worship, all the adoration, all the
honor both now and always.

NOTE

1. Albert E. Day, *An Autobiography of Prayer* (Nashville: The Disciplined Order of Christ, 1952), quoted in Bob Benson, *Disciplines for the Inner Life* (Waco, Tex.: Word, 1985), 53.

CHAPTER 7

∽

GOD'S HOURGLASS

∽

Jesus . . . looked toward heaven and prayed:
"Father, the time has come."

—JOHN 17:1

_Time. Depending upon your perspective it ticks. It plods. It marches. It flies. To a child, thirty minutes edge forward interminably (especially on a car trip). To a maturing adult, decades seem to be added to the fabric of one's experiences in less time than it takes for a Web browser to locate an Internet address.

Time is, after all, neither more nor less than a matter of perspective, more specifically a matter of earthbound perspective.

For centuries mankind's greatest minds have speculated on time, have theorized about its potential to run in subsequent streams or concurrent timelines, have obsessed over our captivity to its relentless passage.

From the heavenly perspective, though, time is simply a convenient invention of an ingenious Creator. Like other elements tied to this fallen, temporal creation, time as we know it will not (pardon the bad pun) stand the test of time. This is true in our individual lives and in creation's countdown clock.

Intuitively, believer and nonbeliever alike recognize the temporary nature of time. For some, this realization leads to the conclusion that they might as well squeeze every ounce of gusto from each moment. This hedonistic, pleasure-seeking path is not only self-destructive (as it leads to all sorts of debauchery), but contrary to biblical principles. The Scriptures are clear that a day of reckoning will come when God calls us to take responsibility for our actions. As lives are subjected to the litmus test of God's standard of holy perfection, the hedonist will be found wanting.

For the Christ-follower, though, the Latin expression *carpe diem* (seize the day) draws us to a different conclusion. Instead of leading us on a selfish path, it challenges us to use every fraction of our allotted time as God would have us do. All of which presupposes that God, in whose hands *time* has its existence, gave us these moments for a purpose that He would be delighted for us to find.

When Jesus opened His address to the Father with the words you read at the beginning of this chapter ("Father, the time has come"), He was acknowledging a fact the Father already knew. (It wasn't news to God that the time of Jesus' sacrifice was drawing near.) Perhaps Jesus vocalized these words for the sake of His followers—to remind them of the theological concept that our time is in God's hands (Daniel 2:21). But it seems more likely that Jesus was adding His own verbal assent to the Father's plan for our salvation, the blueprint Scripture tells us was established before the foundation of the world (Revelation 13:8 NKJV).

It is common for us to quote Jeremiah 29:11 to remind each other that God has a good purpose for our lives, but does that knowledge get beyond the superficial layers of our minds? Does it seep into the core of our hearts? Paul wrote to the Ephesians to explain that although they haven't seen the end of all things with their own eyes, God will accomplish all He has promised "when the times will have reached their fulfillment" (Ephesians 1:10)—in His time and in His way.

Paul continues by reaffirming his readers' (and our) faith: "In him we were also chosen, having been predestined according to the plan of him who works out everything in conformity with the purpose of his will, in order that we, who were the first to hope in Christ, might be for the praise of his glory" (Ephesians 1:11–12). So our times and seasons have the preordained purpose of bringing God glory. What more important task could we have than to bring glory to our Creator and to His Son who paid for our pardon with His lifeblood?

In a Sunday school class I attended this morning, the teacher exhorted us to return to the mission, the ministry, the calling that God has placed on our lives. What she meant was that as God continues to give us time, we continue to need His wisdom in how to spend it. Maybe you haven't strayed from that path. For the rest of us, it may seem that God's call was an eternity ago, that His plan hasn't withstood the pressure time has exerted on it, that it wasn't practical—given the realities of surviving this life. Well, for those in that second category, the time just may have come today for us to return to the forward-moving train of His will.

So, as we approach God in prayer, perhaps an acknowledgment of God's hand on the hourglass of our lives, controlling the sands of time that move through the constricted neck, would be in order. If Jesus felt it necessary to acknowledge the Father's hand in His times and seasons, how much more ought we do the same? It is not news to God that He is Master of time. But it may be news to those of us who have been coasting through time for years on end. I must confess that today it was news to me.

PERSONAL PRAYER STARTER

Creator God,

I realize that time is a tool in Your hands. It may seem uncontrollable to me, but I know that You hold it under control. So now, I think the time is right for me to . . .

I know I tend to get sidetracked, especially when I . . .

But now, I purpose to get back on board the train of Your will for my life. I want to accomplish everything that is in Your plan for my life—no less and no more.

Please make Your plan clear to me. As You reveal it, I will move forward in it.

CHAPTER 8

✵

THE ULTIMATE
LAST WORD

✵

Come, Thou incarnate Word,
Gird on Thy mighty sword,
Our prayer attend!
Come, and Thy people bless,
And give Thy word success,
Spirit of holiness, on us descend.

—"COME, THOU ALMIGHTY KING." (AUTHOR UNKNOWN)

In 1988, I taught a 200-level writing course at my alma mater, Ball State University. When I stepped into that classroom, the students automatically respected me, simply because the university deemed my mastery of the craft sufficient to qualify me to teach them.

In 1999, I began to teach freshman English composition at a local Bible college. In the eleven-year interim something seemed to have happened in the minds of the student population. On the first day of each semester, my current students sit with arms folded, waiting for me to establish my credibility to teach them anything about writing. No matter that I make my living as a writer and have college degrees that qualify me in the eyes of the school's accreditation board, these kids feel differently about authority. It is not something they acknowledge without sufficient proof; it is a privilege they grant capriciously based on personal experience with a faculty member. So, before I go over the syllabus to explain the expectations of the course, I must take time to describe the qualifications I bring to the classroom and establish my credibility.

Why this diatribe on modern youth? Because I think this mindset carries over into the entire fabric of Western society—across generational lines. Authority must be verified by our experience; we confer it neither eagerly nor easily. Not only does it carry over into society, but more critically it seeps into our responses to the mastery, the right to rule, that God bears in our lives.

This is not a new issue. In fact, a recognition of God's authority to superintend human lives was a primary element in Jesus' high priestly prayer. In John 17:2, we hear Jesus say, "For you [Father] granted him [Jesus] authority over all people that he might give eternal life to all those you have given him."

It is an issue that awed the people of Capernaum: "The people were amazed at his teaching, because he taught them as one who had authority, not as the teachers of the law" (Mark 1:22). He was an expert in matters of eternity. And since He had grown up as one of them, they couldn't pinpoint the location of His education. How and when was He transformed from the young boy they had seen growing up in Galilee into this confident young teacher of truth? Where did He earn this authority?

If authority is, as the dictionary defines it, primarily the "power to enforce laws, exact obedience, command, determine, or judge,"[1] from where did Jesus derive this power, this right? Listen as the human rulers challenged the Son of God's authority: "Jesus entered the temple courts, and, while he was teaching, the chief priests and the elders of the people came to him. 'By what authority are you doing these things?' they asked. 'And who gave you this authority?'" (Matthew 21:23). Although Jesus refuses to answer in this case (read the context for His skillful reply), in other contexts we see that Jesus received the authority not only to teach and heal, but also to judge their eternal destinies (John 5:26–27) from the Father. In fact, Scripture tells us "there is no authority except that which God has established" (Romans 13:1).

According to *Nelson's Illustrated Bible Dictionary,* two forms of authority exist: intrinsic authority and derived authority. God the Father is the only One with intrinsic authority, defined as "belonging to one's essential nature." God has this ultimate, overarching authority simply because of who He is. Yahweh. The Great I Am. Any other authority, including that conferred upon the other members of the Holy Trinity (Jesus the Son and the Holy Spirit) flows from the Father. Derived authority (defined as "given to one from another source") is delegated from the Father.[2]

Listen as God reveals Himself to Job, the godly man of antiquity who is famous for the trials he underwent because of his righteousness.

Where were you when I laid the earth's foundation? Tell me, if you understand. Who marked off its dimensions? Surely you know! Who stretched a measuring line across it? On what were its footings set, or who laid its cornerstone—while the morning stars sang together and all the angels shouted for joy? (Job 38:4–7)

Yet, in our audacity, our skeptical, independent natures continue to challenge the Creator God's authority. Maybe not in overt ways; maybe we don't question His right to rule the entire universe, but more likely we challenge His right to superintend the events of our lives—especially when those events seem painful from our temporal point of view.

Read, if you would, Jesus' commission to His followers. He prefaced it by saying, "All authority in heaven and on earth has been given to me. Therefore go and make disciples of all nations" (Matthew 28:18–19). As we recognize His authority in our lives, He confers upon us a limited form of authority, of influence to bring His message to our spheres. Not because of who we are but because of our relationship with Him.

What does this mean to our prayer lives? Jesus admitted early in His prayer that any authority He had came from the Ultimate Source, from His Father. Could it be that this admission of our proper chain of authority in our own prayers makes us willing to see circumstances from God's perspective? Could it be necessary for our quick-to-challenge-authority, twenty-first-century selves to acknowledge that any power we may wield in our little worlds (our homes, our communities, our workplaces) has come only because God has conferred it upon us?

PERSONAL PRAYER STARTER

God of ultimate authority,

I kneel before You. I confess there have been times when, like the skeptics of New Testament times, I have challenged Your authority in my life. For these, I am truly sorry.

Now I lay out before You these areas of my life: . . . I acknowledge Your authority to superintend these issues, and I step aside, asking You to take charge.

Thank You for placing me in authority in my spheres of influence, including . . . Please help me use the authority You have conferred in ways that please You.

NOTES

1. *American Heritage Dictionary,* s.v. "authority."

2. *Nelson's Illustrated Bible Dictionary,* electronic ed. (Nashville: Nelson, 1986), s.v. "authority."

CHAPTER 9

∽

YOUR
KINGDOM COME

∽

The kingdoms of this world—have become
The kingdom of our God and of His Christ
And of His Christ
And He shall reign forever and ever.

—GEORGE FRIDERIC HANDEL (1685–1759), "THE HALLELUJAH CHORUS," *MESSIAH*

If we look at the prayer Jesus modeled for His followers when they asked Him to teach them to pray (Matthew 6), we will see that one of the requests we are to make is that God's kingdom would come on earth as it is in heaven. It is a theme that is evident in John 17, as well. Although Jesus does not specifically use the term "the kingdom of God," He does describe Himself and His followers as being citizens of another world (John 17:16), by implication citizens of the world in which His Father's will is done continuously.

This is a difficult concept for earthbound dwellers to comprehend. We have prayed in this kingdom's authority by rote countless times, and yet, do we know what we are inviting God to do in our realm?

Foremost, we must understand that His is a kingdom of a world invisible to mortals and outside the realm of anything we have experienced earth-side. Jesus pointed this out to the earthly ruler Pontius

Pilate before He was condemned to be crucified. "My kingdom is not of this world," Jesus said. "If it were, my servants would fight to prevent my arrest by the Jews. But now my kingdom is from another place" (John 18:36).

Many times Jesus related the kingdom of His Father in symbols and metaphors to which His astute followers could relate. Remember, the Son of God was the only human who had experienced the fullness of God's kingdom firsthand. Listen to His description in Matthew 13:44–50:

> The kingdom of heaven is like treasure hidden in a field. When a man found it, he hid it again, and then in his joy went and sold all he had and bought that field.
>
> Again, the kingdom of heaven is like a merchant looking for fine pearls. When he found one of great value, he went away and sold everything he had and bought it.
>
> Once again, the kingdom of heaven is like a net that was let down into the lake and caught all kinds of fish. When it was full, the fishermen pulled it up on the shore. Then they sat down and collected the good fish in baskets, but threw the bad away.

As we attempt to comprehend these parables, we must remember Jesus' words to His disciples earlier in this discourse: "The knowledge of the secrets of the kingdom of heaven has been given to you, but not to them [those who don't believe]" (Matthew 13:11). This is why we began this study with a section on how we can know God and believe in His Son as our Savior. Without the kingdom of God within us (as Jesus promised His followers in Luke 17:21), we cannot understand its mysteries.

But what did Jesus mean when He likened His Father's kingdom to a treasure, a pearl, and a net? Or in other Scriptures, when He likened it to a mustard seed (Matthew 13:31) or a small amount of yeast (Matthew 13:33)? These metaphors puzzled me for many years. Commentators don't always agree on their meaning (so the metaphors have puzzled greater minds than mine). But the clearest explanation I could find was in *Nelson's Illustrated Bible Dictionary,* which says,

> The kingdom that comes through the ministry of Jesus dawns in the form of a mystery. Although it is physically present in the deeds and words of Jesus, it does not overwhelm the world. The judgment of God's enemies is postponed. The kingdom that arrived with Jesus . . . arrived secretly like leaven, inconspicuously like a mustard seed, or like a small pearl of great value that can be hidden in one's pocket.[1]

I like the word picture used in this explanation that says God's kingdom didn't overwhelm the world with its power, at least not at Jesus' first coming. As we learned earlier, any authority set up on this earth has been delegated intentionally by God Himself. In fact, His kingdom didn't challenge the authority of Rome or its princes on this earth. The only kingdom whose authority God's kingdom wars against is the counterfeit one Satan set up for himself in intentional opposition to the Creator.

Why did Jesus consider it important that we pray inviting God's kingdom to come? Why did He acknowledge to the Father in His followers' hearing that neither He nor they are of this world? One reason is the war to which we just alluded. *Nelson's Dictionary* points out that "Satan and evil are in retreat now that the kingdom has made its entrance into human history."[2] Not only is a spiritual battle taking place, but we are aligned with the ultimate Victor.

Related to that is the mind-set Christ desires His followers to maintain—one of staying always on the lookout for the pearl of great value, daily pursuing the treasure of His kingdom, spreading His truth through the dough of society like a small amount of yeast.

Will God's kingdom come and His will be done regardless of whether you or I pray for it to be so? Of course. God's will cannot be thwarted; His plan will prevail (Isaiah 55:11). However, as we pray His kingdom into our realm, we have the privilege of participating, of riding the wave of the glorious plans He has for His creation.

PERSONAL PRAYER STARTER

King of kings,
*   With a new understanding, I pray that Your kingdom come*
and Your will be done on earth as it is in heaven.
*   I have requested many things from You over the course of my*
life. Some of my recent requests have included . . .
*   But today I request only that You work in these situations that*
concern me so Your kingdom will be in evidence for the world to see.
*   I bow to Your kingdom and Your wishes in every aspect of my*
life.

NOTES

1. *Nelson's Illustrated Bible Dictionary,* electronic ed. (Nashville: Nelson, 1986), s.v. "Kingdom of God, Kingdom of Heaven."

2. Ibid.

OUR VISION OF GOD

I keep asking that the God of our Lord Jesus Christ,
the glorious Father, may give you the Spirit of wisdom and revelation,
so that you may know him better.

—EPHESIANS 1:17

"I have revealed you to those whom you gave me out of the world" (John 17:6), Jesus told the Father. Why was it important to Jesus' ministry on earth that He reveal the Father to those who are called out of the world to be His followers? Earlier in His high priestly prayer (v. 3), Jesus gave us a hint when He pointed out that the key to eternal life is to know the Father and the Son: "Now this is eternal life: that they may know you, the only true God, and Jesus Christ, whom you have sent."

Since He created humans to walk with Him in the Garden of Eden in the cool of the day, to talk with Him, to be companions with Him, the Father has always wanted us to know Him. To know Him even as He knows us. Intimately. Completely. Unabashedly. According to *Nelson's Illustrated Bible Dictionary,* in Eden "only the humans had one-on-one conscious communion or fellowship with God (Genesis 1:29–30; 2:15–16; 3:8)."[1]

But as we established earlier, sin put an impassible chasm between humans and the holy God. So, when even the godly man Moses wanted to see God, He could not do so, not completely. He could only see the backside of God's glory. And Isaiah, one of the most prolific visionaries God used to foretell the coming of Jesus Christ, upon approaching God's throne, said, "'Woe to me!' I cried. 'I am ruined! For I am a man of unclean lips, and I live among a people of unclean lips, and my eyes have seen the King, the Lord Almighty'" (Isaiah 6:5).

In John 6:46 Jesus tells an unbelieving crowd that He is the only One who has truly known the Father. Making the Father known to us was so pivotal to the purpose of Jesus' life on this earth that when His followers just weren't able to put it all together in their minds, He chided them:

> "If you really knew me, you would know my Father as well. From now on, you do know him and have seen him."
> Philip said, "Lord, show us the Father and that will be enough for us."
> Jesus answered: "Don't you know me, Philip, even after I have been among you such a long time? Anyone who has seen me has seen the Father. How can you say, 'Show us the Father'?" (John 14:7–9)

Practically speaking, how was Jesus able to show us the Father? According to the writer of the letter to the Hebrews, "The Son is the radiance of God's glory and the exact representation of his being" (Hebrews 1:3a). And according to the apostle Paul, "He is the image of the invisible God" (Colossians 1:15a). To those who don't believe in Christ, this truth appears to be blasphemy (Matthew 26:65); but to those who choose to believe, "it is the power of God for the salvation of everyone who believes" (Romans 1:16).

Jesus used everyday means to reveal the Father to us. First, He stayed in constant contact with the Father so He would know those things that the Father wanted Him to do. "I tell you the truth, the Son can do nothing by himself; he can do only what he sees his

Father doing, because whatever the Father does the Son also does" (John 5:19).

Another means was to talk often to His followers about the Father, painting word pictures of what the Father is like—of His character qualities, His love, His mercy. One of the most comforting and exciting revelations Jesus made of His Father was when He told the disciples, "The Father Himself loves you, because you have loved Me, and have believed that I came forth from God" (John 16:27 NKJV). What a concept! The God of the universe loves you and me, because we believe in His Son, Jesus Christ.

Yet another way Jesus taught His followers about His Father was when, in the final moments of His life, He deferred to the Father's will. Remember that when Jesus prayed in the Garden of Gethsemane for the Father's will—rather than His human preference—to be done, the Father's will meant Jesus' physical death. But Jesus modeled for us the picture of a submissive Son by bowing to the Father's plan.

We are privileged, then, that Jesus made the God of the universe known to us mere mortals (John 17:6, 21, 26). We are enlightened as to His character and His personal love for us. And, in watching how Jesus related to His Father, we can imitate His actions, His character qualities, His submissive responses, as we grow in our knowledge of Him. Armed with that knowledge, then, our prayer lives will be transformed. As we bring ourselves before the Father, we will become so attached to Him, so willing to allow Him to work in and through us, that the world will see Him by watching us.

Bible commentator Matthew Henry says our responsibility is to make God plain to everyone we meet. If we give the world a clear vision of God at work in our lives, people will say, "We will go with you, for we see that God is with you."[2]

PERSONAL PRAYER STARTER

Invisible God,
  As I read those things Jesus revealed to His followers about You, I am awed that You want me to know You personally.
  Show me something new about Yourself today. I need to know You as my . . .
  Today I am facing . . .
  Would You reveal to me how You would have me handle these situations, so that those who watch me will catch a glimpse of You at work through my life?
  Thank You, my Father.

NOTES

1. *Nelson's Illustrated Bible Dictionary,* electronic ed. (Nashville: Nelson, 1986) s.v. "image of God."

2. Matthew Henry, *Matthew Henry's Commentary on the Whole Bible,* modern edition database, © 1991 by Hendrickson Publishers Inc., "John 17:20–23 PP22."

CHAPTER 11

JESUS—GOD'S ONE AND ONLY

Thou, O Christ, art all I want,
More than all in Thee I find;
Raise the fallen, cheer the faint,
Heal the sick, and lead the blind.

—CHARLES WESLEY (1707–1788), "JESUS, LOVER OF MY SOUL"

*W*hen I was eight years old, I took my first violin lesson. For twelve years, I continued with lessons, learning from a variety of teachers techniques to refine my skills. To this day, I take an occasional brush-up lesson to work on weak spots. But one thing I've noticed: Regardless of my technique, I need to play an instrument made with quality craftsmanship if my efforts are to sound smooth and mellow and sweet.

So it long has been my dream to play—if only for a moment—an authentic Stradivarius. I have jokingly asked the Lord for a heavenly Strad when I reach paradise.

For several years I cruised pawnshops, looking for a violin with good craftsmanship and tone quality. One day I found one that looked promising. Looking inside the instrument's F holes (the openings in the body that allow sound from the interior to be relayed across a concert hall) I saw a sticker that named the instrument's craftsman. The first word I read on the sticker, in large, fancy hand lettering, was "*Stradivarius.*" Surely it couldn't be. I read further. The sticker actually said, "MADE IN THE TRADITION OF *Stradivarius.*" Quite a difference in meaning. Although it may have been patterned after a Strad, clearly the instrument was a replica, an imitation of the real thing.

I bought the violin, and it turned out to be a nice instrument, worth a few thousand dollars, but nothing like the dream Strad that would have been valued at hundreds of thousands of dollars.

Many things in this world are like that violin—replicas of something great, but not the real thing. The wildly popular PBS program "Antiques Roadshow" has a nice word for phony antiques, designed to deceive uneducated buyers: *reproductions.* We may call them *faux* (foreign words always sound more exotic). But despite our attempts to soften it with our words, the fact remains: A fake is a fake.

When antique experts study their craft, they do not spend the bulk of their preparation looking at forgeries, but rather at the real antiques. They come to know authentic objects so well that when they encounter a fake they immediately recognize even subtle differences from the authentic objects.

What does all of this have to do with our study of prayer? Jesus asked the Father to see that the world would recognize His authenticity, His deity, "that the world may believe that you have sent me," He prayed (John 17:21b). His desire was that the world would recognize that He is the real thing, the true Messiah planted in a virgin's womb by the Spirit of God. Jesus is, after all, the one and only Son of God. Many times in the New Testament, He carries that moniker. For example, the apostle John records these words of the Master, "Whoever believes in him [He is referring to Himself here] is not condemned, but whoever does not believe stands condemned already because he has not believed in the name of God's one and only Son" (John 3:18).

Many people carry the name Joshua (the English equivalent of *Yeshua*—Jesus' Hebrew name) or Jesus; many have claimed to be the long-awaited Messiah from God. But there is only one Jesus Christ, only one whose name will open the gates of heaven to us. Listen to the apostle Peter's words, "Salvation is found in no one else, for there is no other name under heaven given to men by which we must be saved" (Acts 4:12). What is that name? "Jesus Christ of Nazareth" (v. 10).

When we pray in that name, calling upon the rights and privileges purchased for us by His shed blood, Jesus tells us that "the Father will give you whatever you ask in my name" (John 15:16). His authenticity as God's Son, then, affects the most primary element of our prayer life, our privilege to carry on a conversation with the Lord God Almighty.

Recognizing the authenticity of Jesus as God's Son carries with it another benefit that affects the direction of our prayer lives. Much like the forgery experts mentioned earlier, the more time we spend with Christ, the more likely we are to recognize His voice, discerning it from the voice of our own desires, the voice of an imposter, the voice of the tempter.

Listen to Jesus' words on this subject. He likens Himself to the Good Shepherd whose "sheep follow him because they know his voice. But they will never follow a stranger; in fact, they will run away from him because they do not recognize a stranger's voice" (John 10:4b–5). Later in the passage Jesus promises, "My sheep listen to my voice; I know them, and they follow me" (v. 27).

If my prayer life is indeed the "second word" (as we discussed in chapter 3), the response to the First Word—if communication with God is at God's initiative—then I must spend time listening in prayer, silent before God's throne. This is difficult for me, as I am by nature quick to speak and slow to listen. Yet it is crucial to relationship building on any level for me to allow the other party to speak. How much more is this true in my relationship with my Lord. Moments of silence in His presence, after His name has opened the door to me, are filled with priceless jewels of wisdom from His Word if I am practiced enough to discern His voice. How rich that I have Jesus' promise that by spending time allowing Him to lead me like a good shepherd, I will recognize His voice.

What I gain from this practiced recognition of the authentic Son of God is far more valuable than any Stradivarius—whether the earthly or heavenly model.

PERSONAL PRAYER STARTER

———————— ✐ ————————

Father,

I come to You in the name of Jesus Christ. I acknowledge that He is Your one and only Son, and I am grateful that He has given me His name so that I might gain access to You.

I ask that I may recognize Your voice, that I may be able to discern Your words over those from all other sources.

Today, rather than speaking, I choose to sit silently, listening to You speak to my heart through Your Word . . .

Since I have discerned Your voice, I now purpose to follow Your direction.

———————— ✐ ————————

CHAPTER 12

∽

EMBODIMENT OF TRUTH

∽

Search me, O God, and know my heart;
test me and know my anxious thoughts.
See if there is any offensive way in me,
and lead me in the way everlasting.

—PSALM 139:23–24

Set them apart for Your use, Father, using the truth of the words that come from Your mouth to make them worthy of Our holiness. Essentially, that's what Jesus is asking of the Father in John 17:17. We will cover the issue of our cleanliness and worthiness for His use in a later chapter. In this section of our study, we are concerned with those issues of God's character that Jesus prayed for us to make known to the world. So the character quality we examine here is truth.

Truth is so indelibly marked into God's character that Jesus said of Himself, "I am . . . the truth" (John 14:6). *Nelson's Illustrated Bible Dictionary* says, "In the Old and New Testaments, truth is a fundamental moral and personal quality of God. God proclaimed that He is 'merciful and gracious, longsuffering, and abounding in goodness and truth' . . . All Jesus said was true, because He told the truth which He heard from God."[1]

As I listened to a singer last evening, he ended one set of songs with a supposedly humorous lyric that bragged about a character who was the greatest liar who ever lived. The crowd laughed along. I suppose that is to be expected in our society, where our leaders flaunt their falsehood, redefine words when their untruths are exposed, and defy the truth by continuing to lie even after being caught in their duplicity.

Jesus was strong in His opposition to falsehood. Listen to His acerbic words to those who would not believe the truths He preached: "You belong to your father, the devil, and you want to carry out your father's desire. He was a murderer from the beginning, not holding to the truth, for there is no truth in him. When he lies, he speaks his native language, for he is a liar and the father of lies. Yet because I tell the truth, you do not believe me!" (John 8:44–45).

A world more likely to follow the father of lies than the Son of Truth asks with Pontius Pilate at Jesus' sham trial, "What is truth?" (John 18:38). We might as well be asking "What is God?" as truth is inseparable from who He is.

If I had been in Pilate's shoes, would I have recognized the Truth who stood before me? Would I have plumbed the depths of Truth, or would I have considered the Truth an inconvenience to the stability of my power base? Would I have condemned Truth to death to simplify my own life?

Truthfully, what would you have done? Perhaps a better question would be, in daily life, what do we do with the truth, small t and capital T?

A little blonde doll sits on my bookshelf. The doll holds no intrinsic value; she is a dime-store special my mom rescued from my garage sale pile last year. Her name is Baby Trueheart. My father bought her for me when I was seven or eight. She marks a special event in my life, an occasion when I had opportunity to make my life temporarily easier by not telling the truth, not taking responsibility for something I had done wrong, a time when no one would have been the wiser. But, as a young Christian, I determined to heed the Holy Spirit's prompting in my heart to take the consequences of my wrong rather than covering it with a lie—adding wrong to wrong. I confessed my deed, willing to take whatever punishment I had earned. For telling the truth when I didn't have to, my dad rewarded me with little Trueheart—a tangible reminder that it is always right to tell the truth.

We may define truth by what it is not; we may say it is the opposite of that which is false. This is simpler to maintain, as it may satisfy our partially seared consciences. We may then hide behind the fact that technically we spoke no falsehood, even though we may have kept silent when given the opportunity to set an untruth right. This definition is incomplete. Recall the oath that witnesses in a courtroom take. They promise to tell "the truth, the whole truth, and nothing but the truth." Leaving nothing left unsaid; failing to embellish the facts with any falsehoods. This is truth.

When Jesus was incarnated on this globe, the apostle John described Him as "full of grace and truth" (John 1:14). Not just bearing a little truth, but full to overflowing with the character quality of truth. His truth, though, is not the harsh variety. His truth is tempered by His grace. Balanced by it. Inseparable from it. The writers of *Vine's Expository Dictionary of Biblical Words* explain that when the New Testament uses the Greek words we translate as truth, "the meaning is not merely ethical 'truth,' but 'truth' in all its fullness and scope, as embodied in [Christ]; He was the perfect expression of the truth . . . not merely verbal, but sincerity and integrity of character."[2]

When Jesus was readying His followers for His physical departure, He promised to send the third person of the Trinity to lead them into all truth. Jesus called the name of this individual "the Spirit of Truth" (John 16:13). Of all the character qualities Jesus could have used to describe His counterpart (love, holiness, justice, or jealousy—for starters), He chose truth. It is, then, the Holy Spirit's action in our lives to use God's Word to reveal truth and thus to make us clean and pure for use in God's service. The Spirit of Truth breathes life into the truth of God's Word, thus empowering it to change our lives.

So, now, as we confront truth and "the Truth" in our prayer lives, we have a choice. We can respond to the Holy Spirit's prompting, allowing the Truth to cleanse us, or we can be like Pilate, pushing the truth aside as we attempt to maximize our own convenience. The truth is there before each of us, but will we acknowledge it, own it, take its consequences for our own?

PERSONAL PRAYER STARTER

──────────── ✐ ────────────

Father of truth,

Thank You that you are the Truth. As I have come to understand the importance truth carries in Your sight, I come before You now to acknowledge the truth about who I am.

I acknowledge that I am . . .

I also acknowledge those untruthful things I have said and done, those truths I have left unsaid. Things like . . .

I thank You for the forgiveness and cleansing You offer when I own the truth about myself. I ask that the Spirit of Truth would search me and make me worthy for Your use.

──────────── ✐ ────────────

NOTES

1. *Nelson's Illustrated Bible Dictionary,* electronic ed. (Nashville: Nelson, 1986), s.v. "truth."

2. *Vine's Expository Dictionary of Biblical Words,* electronic ed. (Nashville: Nelson, 1997), s.v. "true, truly, truth."

CHAPTER 13

SPENDING FOREVER WHERE JESUS IS

To Thee, great One in Three,
Eternal praises be, hence evermore.
Thy sovereign majesty, may we in glory see,
And to eternity love and adore.
—"COME, THOU ALMIGHTY KING" (AUTHOR UNKNOWN)

*H*ave you ever tried to imagine *forever?* I have. Late at night, as a small child, I tried to picture eternity.

On many occasions, having just knelt with my mother and prayed, I would be lying awake in my bed still thinking about God. Perhaps I had been reading a Bible story about living forever with Him. Perhaps I had been listening to a song about God having lived in heaven for eternity past, present, and future. Whatever it was, I would lie there thinking about what forever would be like.

No beginning. No end. Going on and on and on and . . .

Suddenly, my palms would get sweaty, my heart would pound, my mouth would get dry. I would be, in those moments, paralyzed with panic. I had reached the limits of my understanding; my mind wasn't big enough to comprehend anything or anyone who had neither a beginning nor an end. I am, after all, limited in my context by

the temporal. All of us who are earth-dwellers are under the tyranni-
cal jurisdiction and limitations of time.

Although I now know enough of God that I am no longer paralyzed with fear, my adult mind is no closer to imagining eternity
than I was all those years ago. I am no less amazed at the God who
always was and always will be than I was when I was a child. Nothing caused Him to come into being; He simply is.

When Moses asked God, "What is your name?" God's reply was
"I Am" (Exodus 3:14). It is a name that encompasses the past, present, and future. Not "I Was," not "I Will Be," but in the present as I
have always been and as I will always be—the "I Am" never changes.
He is constant. He has always been love, and He will continue to be.
He has always been faithful to His people, and He will continue to
be. He has always been truth, and He will continue to be.

Again, I have nothing and no one to compare to Him. He is the
only One with no beginning and no end. When the glorified Christ
described Himself to the apostle John, He put it in terms that were
slightly more understandable in a human context. He said, "I am
the Alpha and the Omega . . . who is, and who was, and who is to
come, the Almighty" (Revelation 1:8).

And again in Revelation 22:13 He explains for those of us who
may not be familiar with the Greek alphabet, "I am the Alpha and
the Omega, the First and the Last, the Beginning and the End." He
was the "I Am" at the beginning of time as we know it, and as
human history on this planet closes (at an undisclosed time) He will
continue to be the same.

What does it mean to us to have a changeless, eternal God? In
practical terms, it means that once we know His character (a discovery that will continue to reveal new layers of truth to us every day),
we can be assured that He will never change, He will never be anything other than what He is. He is the one constant in a world of
earthquakes, hurricane-force winds, divorce, death, and the rise and
fall of nations. Though everything around us may change, we can
depend upon Him to be "the same yesterday and today and forever"
(Hebrews 13:8).

As Jesus continued praying for you and me, He reminded the Father that His ultimate desire was that we might be where He is (John 17:24). Our togetherness with Him would not be temporal, but eternal. Forever with Jesus: That is the hope of the believer. It is the hope that the apostle Paul was persuaded Jesus was able to keep safe for him until the day when it would come to fruition (2 Timothy 1:12). This hope—my hope—is not just based upon the promised physical beauty of heaven, but upon the assurance that heaven is where my Lord and Savior will be. Streets of gold and gates of priceless gems may be permanent features of that celestial city where we will live some day, but the real treasure (the pearl of great price) is being together with Jesus for time without end—for always.

Even more exciting than the fact that I can hardly wait to get to that place where, as the hymnist wrote, "faith shall be sight"[1] is that Jesus Himself longs for me to be where He is. Overhear the conversation between our Lord and His Father: "I want those you have given me to be with me where I am" (John 17:24).

This is love. First, that He chose to weave eternity into human souls. That He created us for eternal fellowship with Him. And then that He wanted us to be with Him so much that He laid down His life to make it possible—after we humans had disqualified ourselves from fellowship with Him by choosing to sin.

Eternity in heaven, at the feet of the "I Am," "lost in wonder, love and praise."[2] That will be paradise.

But it is a paradise I don't want to keep to myself. I want to share it with others. The implication to my life of this element of Jesus' prayer is clear to me. I want those I encounter in this world, those I come to care about, those I learn to love—I want them all to be in heaven where Jesus is, as well. So, my prayer is not for myself alone, but that my colleagues, my family members, my friends and acquaintances might all spend forever where Jesus is—and where I will be.

PERSONAL PRAYER STARTER

Alpha and Omega, eternal King, who was and is and is to come,
    With the hymn writer I am "lost in wonder, love and praise"
at the promise of spending forever with You. And I add my voice in
thankfulness by saying . . .
    Now I pray that You will help me share this wonderful eterni-
ty with those I love and care for. I especially pray for . . . and ask
that You will give me the opportunity to tell them about Your offer of
forgiveness for sin and Your desire to spend eternity with them.
    Thank You for this privilege.

NOTES

1. Horatio G. Spafford (1828–88), "It is Well with My Soul."
2. Charles Wesley (1707–88), "Love Divine All Loves Excelling."

CHAPTER 14

TO KNOW HIM IS
TO WORSHIP HIM

Were the whole realm of nature mine,
That were a present far too small:
Love so amazing, so divine,
Demands my soul, my life, my all.

—ISAAC WATTS (1674–1748), "WHEN I SURVEY THE WONDROUS CROSS"

Since we don't serve kings and we are not frequently tempted to bow in adoration to our elected officials—whose failings and foibles are broadcast across the evening's headlines—the concept of worship is largely lost on our generation. Historically, however, kings expected their subjects to worship them: to pay them homage, to expound often on their greatness and worthiness to rule, to express admiration, awe, and respect.

Even in our day, think of all the protocols one must go through to see a human dignitary. We would first petition the dignitary's "people" for an audience. To be granted such, we must have a valid purpose for the meeting. Our self-importance notwithstanding, we would not be given the latitude to chat indiscriminately with one of great power and consequence. We must be willing to travel to where the dignitary is; he won't come to us. We must prepare ourselves, dressing appropriately for the occasion; it is likely we would submit to a security inspection prior to being brought into his presence.

How does this scenario compare with our entry into the presence of the Dignitary above all dignitaries? The almighty God, the great I Am, deserves infinitely more worship than any human ruler ever could expect or demand. And yet, too often we degrade our vision of God—we make Him into someone we can fully relate to, someone we can manipulate for our own purposes. We make Him our buddy, our sugar daddy, or our genie. This is a travesty.

When Jesus prayed that we would see the Father's glory and His own true glory (John 17:24), how did He expect us to respond to that unparalleled revelation? Every individual in Scripture who had a direct encounter with the Almighty (or who even caught a glimpse of His back as He passed by, as did Moses in Exodus 33) bowed in deference, awe, and wonder. When Moses asked to see God's glory, he was told, "I will cause all my goodness to pass in front of you, and I will proclaim my name, the Lord, in your presence. . . . But," God said, "you cannot see my face, for no one may see me and live" (Exodus 33:19–20).

Moses' response to seeing the back of God's glory? "Moses bowed to the ground at once and worshiped" (Exodus 34:8). Some translations say Moses fell to the ground in worship.

Yes, Jesus told His disciples that He would no longer call them servants, but rather they would be His friends. And yes, His death made a way for us to come and go freely in God's presence. But there is a flip side to this freedom. We can't forget whose presence we are approaching. And we can't forget the immeasurable price God's Son paid to make this relationship possible.

In his book on worship in the church, Donald Hustad comments on the complexity of who God is to the believer:

God is at one and the same time our Creator, Redeemer (through Jesus Christ), Sustainer, Indweller (by the Holy Spirit), Friend, and Judge. It helps to remember that we approach God individually as a created one, a redeemed one, a sustained one, an indwelt one, a befriended one, and a judged one.[1]

Let's return to the example of the apostle John: the beloved disciple who laid his head on Jesus' breast, who on this earth never was far from His special friend Jesus. John was one of the Master's inner circle. Where Jesus went, John went alongside. He followed in good times and bad. At Jesus' Triumphal Entry into Jerusalem, John was there; at His trial before the high priest, John stood by watching; and at His crucifixion, John was close enough to receive a final directive from Jesus: "Here is your mother" (John 19:27). Truly, if anyone qualified as a friend of Jesus, it was John.

Yet when John encountered the glorified Christ, first on the Mount of Transfiguration (Matthew 17) and then in the book of Revelation, he was dumbstruck. He fell at Jesus' feet in fear and trembling. Yes, Jesus was the same friend he had known on earth. But when John came face to face with the Glory, he knew his place—not as buddy but as worshiper. Like John before us, when we approach God in prayer, we understand our insignificance in light of His awesome majesty.

Must we physically bow our knees as we approach His throne in prayer? Not necessarily. Scripture includes examples of those who bowed, but also of those who stood in the congregation to worship. Outward posture is far less important than the inward acknowledgment of the awesome character of God.

Several years ago, vocalist Cynthia Clawson began her concerts with a moving a cappella rendition of the great hymn by Walter Chalmers Smith, "Immortal, Invisible, God Only Wise." Cynthia's clear soprano voice would echo through the concert hall announcing the truth about God: "Most blessed, most glorious, the Ancient of Days, Almighty, victorious, Thy great name we praise." With these words, she set the tone for the hour, she invited God to be present, and she asked the audience to participate in acknowledging Him in collective worship.

The language of this hymn may seem archaic, yet its content is a marvelous setting for our understanding of the God to whom we pray. God is all the hymn describes—and much more: glorious, eternal, almighty, victorious, and worthy of our praise. So, as we enter His presence daily, as He beckons us to catch brief new glimpses of His glory, let's carry with us not only our petitions, but also our heartfelt worship. After all, the more we know of Him, the more reasons we have to worship Him.

PERSONAL PRAYER STARTER

My Lord and my God,
    You are far beyond my human understanding. And yet You have invited me into Your presence.
    I ask now for a glimpse, a new respect and awe for Your qualities of . . .
    Let me see You as . . .
    All this I ask, that I may learn to bow before You in the respect and deference Your majesty deserves.

NOTE
1. Donald P. Hustad, *Jubilate II* (Carol Stream, Ill.: Hope Publishing, 1993), 99.

PART THREE

Our Personal INTERESTS

Now that we have a clearer
understanding of the majesty of the
One to whom we pray, we can carry
our every concern to His loving arms.

CHAPTER 15

WHATEVER THE NEED

All the way my Savior leads me,
Cheers each winding path I tread,
Gives me grace for ev'ry trial,
Feeds me with the living Bread.

—FANNY J. CROSBY (1820–1915), "ALL THE WAY MY SAVIOR LEADS ME."

So far, we have learned about the character of God and about how to pray in line with the priorities He holds. Now it is appropriate for us to turn our attention toward the needs we have in our individual lives. These are the issues for which we pray regularly already. However, it behooves us to reexamine our prayer patterns in light of what we have come to understand about the God to whom we pray.

Certainly we are correct to pray regularly, asking the Lord to provide for our needs. Even Jesus acknowledged that all that has been provided comes from the Father's hand when He said, "Everything you have given me comes from you" (John 17:7). And just before He broke into His high priestly prayer, He told His disciples to make their requests of the Father in His name. I like the way *The Living Bible* paraphrases the instruction: "Then you will present your petitions over my signature! And I won't need to ask the Father to grant you these requests, for the Father himself loves you dearly because you love me and believe that I came from the Father" (John 16:26–27 TLB).

Remembering what we have learned about His character, we realize that our Father desires our best. Recognizing His superiority to us in every way and His benevolent superintendence of our lives, we can acknowledge (even if begrudgingly) that He knows our needs far better than we.

It is a principle woven throughout history: From the earliest days of creation, the Creator provided for the needs of the created. On the sixth day of creation, God made this pronouncement of His provision:

> I give you every seed-bearing plant on the face of the whole earth and every tree that has fruit with seed in it. They will be yours for food. And to all the beasts of the earth and all the birds of the air and all the creatures that move on the ground—everything that has the breath of life in it—I give every green plant for food. (Genesis 1:29–30)

The needs of mankind, before the Fall, were simple. God would sustain them physically with food from the earth and spiritually with His presence (He walked and talked with them in the garden in the cool of the day).

When the humans chose to sin, God's character remained unchanged, even if the needs of His creatures became more complex— and more costly. "The Lord God made garments of skin for Adam and his wife and clothed them" (Genesis 3:21). This provision required the slaying of an animal. God provided not only outward covering of their bodies, but a way of covering their sins, pointing to the ultimate removal of sin in Christ. Speaking to the serpent, He proclaimed the coming of the Messiah: "And I will put enmity between you and the woman, and between your offspring and hers; he will crush your head, and you will strike his heel" (Genesis 3:15).

Later, when God provided a ram for Abraham's sacrifice on Mount Moriah (in place of sacrificing the promised son, Isaac), Abraham marked the spot with the name Jehovah-Jireh (Genesis 22:14 KJV). Interestingly, this is the only place in Scripture that uses this name for God. Most modern translators choose to render Jehovah-Jireh as "The Lord Will Provide"; however, a look back at the original Hebrew word translated as "provide," *ra'ah,* carries the more precise meaning of "The Lord Who Sees."[1]

This should bring us great comfort, as the One who offers to meet whatever need is at hand sees the circumstance perfectly and completely. Listen to one commentator's explanation: "Yahweh sees the needs of those who come to worship before Him on Zion, and there 'is seen,' i.e., reveals Himself to them by answering their prayers and supplying their wants."[2]

This interpretation is consistent with Jesus' New Testament teaching:

> So do not worry, saying, "What shall we eat?" or "What shall we drink?" or "What shall we wear?" For the pagans run after all these things, and your heavenly Father knows that you need them. But seek first his kingdom and his righteousness, and all these things will be given to you as well. (Matthew 6:31–33)

Our priorities, then, can be aligned with His priorities. We need not "run after" the worries of this world, because our Father already sees our need. (In fact, He sees all the needs we will ever have.) We can make our requests known to God in the way that the apostle Paul instructs the Philippian believers: "Do not be anxious about anything, but in everything, by prayer and petition, with thanksgiving, present your requests to God. And the peace of God, which transcends all understanding, will guard your hearts and your minds in Christ Jesus" (4:6–7).

We can rest peacefully and securely in the knowledge that the One who sees is the One who provides. He is always superintending, working in ways I would have no way of seeing, combining diverse resources to provide the financial means, spiritual assets, strength, and courage I need to face each day.

I could give dozens of testimonies that would bespeak His provision, even if I limited myself only to the way He has provided writing projects, enthusiastic encouragers, and (here was a real need) income on my journey of self-employment. But another circumstance of His provision is fresh in my mind.

One Thursday morning, as I exited the college classroom where I teach, I bumped right into a friend I hadn't seen in months, Nancy. Recently retired, Nancy was helping the college organize a rummage sale. Only God knew that I was struggling to focus my mind and heart to work on an early section of this book. God also knew that Nancy is a prayer giant. So, amidst the old furniture and used appliances of the sale, Nancy and I talked. I had barely mentioned my need when she willingly offered to pray me through the writing. When only God knew that I had been feeling vulnerable, in need of someone (outside my own family) to come alongside in prayer for this project, God provided a partner in the work—God provided Nancy.

Whatever your need today, be assured that your Father in heaven sees, He understands, and consistent with His character down through history, He *will* provide.

PERSONAL PRAYER STARTER

Jehovah-Jireh,
    With no preliminaries, I come with my requests, laying them before You and trusting You to provide for my needs. Particularly, today I am concerned about . . .
    I know that You already knew my concerns, but it helps me to carry them to You and entrust the outcomes to You. I trust that You will . . .
    And so, over the signature of Your Son Jesus Christ, I leave these needs with You. Thank You for seeing and for providing.

NOTES

1. *Strong's Greek and Hebrew Dictionary, Bible Soft's New Exhaustive Strong's Numbers and Concordance with Expanded Greek–Hebrew Dictionary* © 1994 Biblesoft International Bible Translators, Inc., s.v. "Jehovah-Jireh."

2. *International Standard Bible Encyclopaedia,* Electronic Database, © 1996 by Biblesoft, s.v. "Jehovah-Jireh."

❦

THE CHOICE TO OWN OR DISOWN

❦

Take away our bent to sinning;
Alpha and Omega be;
End of faith, as its Beginning,
Set our hearts at liberty.

—CHARLES WESLEY (1707–88), "LOVE DIVINE ALL LOVES EXCELLING"

*A*s I write, it is Maundy Thursday. It is late evening. I find myself imagining myself back two millennia, eavesdropping on the scene in the Upper Room, where Jesus spoke comfortingly to His disciples, where He served them by washing their feet, where He fulfilled the Scriptures before their eyes by completing the Passover meal, drinking from the sacred Messiah's cup. Likely Jesus was praying His high priestly prayer about the same hour that I'm writing this.

Then, like a videotape, I fast-forward the scene. Past the agony of the Gethsemane prayer. Past the indignity of His arrest. Past the forced march in the frigid night air to the court of the high priest. And I see Peter. Admirably, he followed, not deserting the Savior whom he was powerless to protect. Relive the scene with me, as narrated by Dr. Luke:

A servant girl saw him seated there in the firelight. She looked closely at him and said, "This man was with him." But he denied it. "Woman, I don't know him," he said.

A little later someone else saw him and said, "You also are one of them."

"Man, I am not!" Peter replied.

About an hour later another asserted, "Certainly this fellow was with him, for he is a Galilean."

Peter replied, "Man, I don't know what you're talking about!" Just as he was speaking, the rooster crowed. The Lord turned and looked straight at Peter. Then Peter remembered the word the Lord had spoken to him: "Before the rooster crows today, you will disown me three times." And he went outside and wept bitterly. (Luke 22:56–62)

I ache for Peter because of this disappointing scene. It must have taken quite an emotional upheaval for Peter to deny Christ. Can you imagine the grief and remorse that would cause that burly, muscular, rough fisherman to sink to the depths of weeping? Not just weeping, but *bitter,* grievous weeping. Tears that would not quench the pain. Tears of shame that he really was no better than the rest, despite his pledge to stand by the Savior even if all the others deserted. But, probably more by instinct than by conscious choice, self-preservation kicked in. And Peter found himself too afraid to own Christ, even to a lowly servant—and a girl at that.

Before we become too pious, blaming Peter, believing the fiction that had we been there, we would have stood nose to nose with Caiaphas himself, not to mention a harmless little servant girl, defending our Lord to the death, let's really put ourselves in Peter's sandals. I am afraid that in reality, our resolve to stand with Christ folds under far less pressure.

Still not convinced? You do know, of course, that while you are basking in your eternity of light, joy, and peace, everyone you encounter on this earth who doesn't have a personal relationship with Christ is doomed to an eternity of constant torture. So, when you meet someone who doesn't know Christ, what do you do? What do you say to your supervisor, teacher, neighbor, friend? Have you openly, before all these witnesses, confessed your relationship with Christ, explained it, lived it out with your actions, made it so plain that they are drawn to pursue this priceless relationship for themselves?

When Jesus prayed for His disciples, this was a major concern for Him. *The Living Bible* makes it so clear: "My prayer for all of them is that they will be of one heart and mind, just as you and I are, Father—that just as you are in me and I am in you, so they will be in us, and the world will believe you sent me" (John 17:21 TLB). We will discuss the issue of unity in later chapters, but for now let's look at the fact that our Lord expects us to be unashamed of our association with Him.

Just as with Peter in the eyes of those around the courtyard fire, Jesus prayed that there would be something about our actions, the way we respect each other, the love we have for each other, the way we sound, the traces of heaven in our speech, that everyone we encounter will identify us with Him. This is not for our own sake, but for His—for the expansion of His kingdom, for the salvation of souls who will be convinced by our actions that He is Someone worth knowing.

Why do I include this matter of prayer in the section where we are considering prayers that are in our own best interest? The best answer I can offer comes straight from the mouth of the Savior: "Whoever acknowledges me before men, I will also acknowledge him before my Father in heaven. But whoever disowns me before men, I will disown him before my Father in heaven" (Matthew 10:32–33).

Whoa! Even in the extreme circumstance where we might be taking our earthly lives or careers in our hands by acknowledging Christ (I once turned a supervisor against me when I confronted her about the way her lifestyle displeased Christ), what are a few years of time in light of standing before God's throne with Jesus by our side, acknowledging us as His own? Conversely, what if we succumb to the pressure of the human powers around us and deny (or even hide our association with) Christ? Is it worth having the Master disown us before His Father?

We must, then, make this a matter of frequent, fervent prayer: that the Father will give us the desire, the courage, the opportunity to stand up for Him in a world that by and large belongs to the enemy of our souls. We must pray that when tested, we will claim Him unashamedly.

PERSONAL PRAYER STARTER

Lord God,

I am ashamed. I have been quick to judge others, such as Your servant Peter, for disowning You, and yet I am guilty of the same transgression. Please forgive me for the opportunities to own You that I have missed—by choice or by default. I think especially of the time when . . .

I also am ashamed of the times when I have not only failed to own You, but by my actions or my words I have either disowned You or brought shame to Your reputation. Those times when . . .

I ask for another opportunity, Lord, to own You before men and women. I ask for the courage, the strength, the words, and the wisdom to acknowledge You, so that others will know the truth about You and me.

Thank You for giving me another chance to serve You.

❦

CARRYING OTHERS TO GOD'S THRONE

❦

May the God of hope fill you with all joy and peace
as you trust in him, so that you may overflow with hope
by the power of the Holy Spirit.

—ROMANS 15:13

I pray for them," Jesus said. "I am not praying for the world, but for those you have given me, for they are yours. . . . I pray also for those who will believe in me through their message" (John 17:9, 20b).

I pray for them. That You would purify them, make them clean so that they can come into Your presence.

I pray for them. That You will keep them safe from the wiles of the enemy of their souls.

I pray for them. That You would unify them and use them to draw others to Yourself.

I pray for them. That You would endow them with Your power and a taste of Your glory.

I pray for them. That You would one day bring them together with Me, to live where I am forever. All this and more *I pray for them.*

What a comfort that when God prayed, He prayed for you and me. When He wept and sweated drops of blood in the Garden of Gethsemane, it was for the sins and betrayals and sickness and death of you and me—and of those we love. When He carried the weight of the world on His shoulders on Calvary, He still prayed for all of us, who because of our individual guilt were participants in the drama of nailing God's Son to the cross of shame. At that moment He prayed, "Father, forgive them, for they do not know what they are doing" (Luke 23:34). Yes, it was a prayer immediately for those in the crowd who were jeering and for those in the Roman battalion who physically pounded nails through His flesh. Yet the prayer still echoes through history. When Jesus carried the weight of our sin, He bore our ignorance of the ways of God as well. So He petitioned God for our forgiveness.

Now that we have accepted that offer of forgiveness, the responsibility for interceding—for bringing others' needs to God's attention—is one we carry on our frail shoulders. "I urge you, first of all," the apostle Paul wrote to his spiritual son Timothy, "to pray for all people. As you make your requests, plead for God's mercy upon them, and give thanks" (1 Timothy 2:1 NLT). Or, as the translators of the *New International Version* put it, "I urge . . . that requests, prayers, intercession and thanksgiving be made for everyone."

What is it that we are to request for others? In Jesus' high priestly prayer, as well as at other times in the Gospels, we hear His priorities in prayer for those He loves. He prays more for our spiritual health and growth than for our physical needs. He prays for our unity, our protection from temptation, our love for one another. In short, He prays for us in those weak areas of our lives that are most in need of His miracle-working, supernatural power.

Let's carry this thought through into our own prayers. Many of us who have gone beyond the first wobbly childlike steps of prayer have added others' requests to our prayer lists. I carry with me, in my *Believer's Life System*™ planner, a prayer list—a reminder of those people and those situations I have promised to remember before the Father. Some items on that list are requests for myself.

Others move to the second concentric circle outward, to the interests of my loved ones, family, friends, and church. Occasionally, I add a few names of missionaries or national church leaders to the list, because I know it would please God for me to pray for other members of the body of Christ. Mostly, though, I pray for those I know and care about; because I care about them, it is natural for me to carry them before God's throne.

Sometimes, I pray for them to be delivered from sickness, to be protected in their travels, to be blessed and directed in their work. I pray for their marriages (and for any potential husband for me who might be out there), for the health of their children, and for the salvation of those who do not yet know Christ personally. But when I read Paul's letters to the believers in the New Testament, I see that if I have a vibrant relationship with Christ, I will pray a much greater blessing upon those I love.

I pray for you. "That God our Father and the Lord Jesus Christ will give each of you his fullest blessings, and his peace in your hearts and your lives" (Philippians 1:2 TLB).

I pray for you. "That the God of our Lord Jesus Christ, the glorious Father, may give you the Spirit of wisdom and revelation, so that you may know him better" (Ephesians 1:17).

I pray for you. "That you may be active in sharing your faith" (Philemon 6).

I pray for you. "That you will not do anything wrong" (2 Corinthians 13:7).

I see something else modeled in the apostle Paul's letters, a continuation of the command we noted earlier that we are to pray for all people. He specifies that we should pray "for kings and all those in authority" (1 Timothy 2:2). So, in a third concentric circle, I am to expand my world of prayer beyond myself, beyond my loved ones and fellow believers, to the world at large—to those decision makers whose choices affect all activity on this globe. I am to petition God with specific requests for those in authority over me in my workplace or school, for civic leaders, for lobbyists, for people who serve in appointed positions in our government, as well as for elected officials. This requires that I become educated about choices these people are facing and that I pray in accordance with God's will for each of them, just as Paul did.

We, then, are to petition God on behalf of everyone—those we know and love, those we know and have a difficult time loving, and those we've never met but know by reputation. Everyone.

Although I may never have met you, you are part of that "everyone." So now I pray for you, echoing Paul's prayer in Ephesians 3:17, *I pray Christ will be more and more at home in your heart as you learn to trust Him.*

PERSONAL PRAYER STARTER

Heavenly Father,

Thank You that even at the moment of Your Son's greatest human crisis, He prayed for me. I am awed by a love like that.

I want to model my own life by His example. So, I bring before You these loved ones . . .

I ask You to meet their earthbound needs, but also their spiritual needs for . . .

Now, I carry before You these individuals who are in authority over me . . . May You reveal Yourself to them as You have done for me.

CHAPTER 18

ఇ⁊

KEEP ME SAFE

ఇ⁊

I've seen the lightning flashing, I've heard the thunder roll.
I've felt sin's breakers dashing, which almost conquered my soul;
I've heard the voice of my Savior, bidding me still to fight on.
He promised never to leave me, never to leave me alone!
—"NEVER ALONE" (AUTHOR UNKNOWN)

*J*esus was duly concerned with the protection of those entrusted to Him—the disciples who walked with Him and those of us who would believe because of their report. Listen to this selection of intercessory verses from His prayer in John 17:

> Holy Father, protect them by the power of your name (11b).
> While I was with them, I protected them and kept them safe by that name you gave me (12a).
> My prayer is not that you take them out of the world but that you protect them from the evil one (15).

Despite Jesus' requests to His Father for the protection of the disciples, of the eleven who were present for that prayer, ten were martyred in gruesome deaths; and the recorder of the prayer, John the Beloved, died at an old age in exile. Hebrews 11 chronicles more of the terrible mistreatment of believers, from Old Testament days and the church age: "Some faced jeers and flogging, while still others were chained and put in prison. They were stoned; they were sawed in two; they were put to death by the sword. They went about in sheepskins and goatskins, destitute, persecuted and mistreated— the world was not worthy of them" (vv. 36–38a).

And what of us, today? What of fellow believers in Muslim and Communist countries who are martyred for their faith? What of a high school student in Columbine, Colorado, who stood up for her faith and was shot dead by fellow students in cold blood? What of a pastor driving to Milwaukee, Wisconsin, whose six children were burned to death before his eyes when a truck lost part of its load and metal sheared through the fuel line of the van in which his family was riding? What of believers whose cancer causes them to totter between life and death sustained only by a morphine drip, or of those who lose their faculties to the aloneness of Alzheimer's disease?

Did the Father fail to answer Jesus' multiple requests for His followers' safety? Was Jesus *not* praying according to the Father's will? My inclination is to say no on both counts. We already have established that Jesus was so attuned to the desires of the Father that He was always operating in the center of the Father's purposes. And if Jesus is truly God, then the sweeping statement attributed to God in Isaiah 55:11—"So shall My word be which goes forth from My mouth; it shall not return to Me empty, without accomplishing what I desire, and without succeeding in the matter for which I sent it" (NASB)—is true of Christ's words, as well. Christ's words always succeed in the matter for which He sends them.

Perhaps, then, we need a clearer understanding of what Christ meant when He prayed for our protection. *The Living Bible* clarifies by paraphrasing verse 15 to read, "I'm not asking you to take them out of the world, but to keep them safe from Satan's power." I don't think Jesus was praying that the evils of this world would never harm our physical bodies. That would be contrary to that which Jesus taught elsewhere, when He said, "He makes His sun rise on the evil and on the good, and sends rain on the just and on the unjust" (Matthew 5:45 NKJV). He meant that good happens to bad people. If that is true, then the converse is also true: Bad happens to good people in this fallen world (see 5:10–12; 10:16–22). Justice will come in the end; yet some of us, like the ancient patriarch Job, will find this world a place of unjustified, if temporary, suffering. The protection for which Jesus prayed was not a brand that would keep us from suffering, but instead the spiritual protection only God could give—the protection of our eternal souls, of our personal relationship with Him, of our eventual destiny after this life's work is over. Listen to the assuring words of the apostle Paul—who was in the midst of torture and intense physical suffering for preaching the gospel: "And that is why I am suffering here in prison. But I am not ashamed of it, for I know the one in whom I trust, and I am sure that he is able to guard what I have entrusted to him until the day of his return" (2 Timothy 1:12 NLT).

Perhaps this statement of Jesus to Simon Peter, recorded in Luke 22, will clarify the concept further. "Simon, Simon, Satan has asked to sift you as wheat. But I have prayed for you, Simon, that your faith may not fail" (vv. 31–32a). We know that Peter did fail Christ, denying Him before men, and yet Christ offered forgiveness and a new commission for Peter to carry out: "Therefore go and make disciples of all nations, baptizing them in the name of the Father and of the Son and of the Holy Spirit, and teaching them to obey everything I have commanded you. And surely I will be with you always, to the very end of the age" (Matthew 28:19–20).

So Jesus' prayer was that the Father would protect Peter's soul from the wiles of the enemy, that when the enemy desired to sift him like wheat, God's power would keep him faithful to Him. Perhaps that is the same kind of protection we ought to request of God for ourselves.

I know that I am much more apt to pray that God would keep all bad things from befalling me—that my life would be soft, cushy, and smooth. God knows constant insulation from sorrows and sufferings is not in my (or His kingdom's) best interest. In the crucible, in the sifting, I learn more about His love and His character.

Although I am fighting through painful circumstances in this world, my Father holds my soul safe in His mighty hands. He has never left me alone—and that's all the protection I will ever need.

PERSONAL PRAYER STARTER

Mighty God,

I have often prayed for my own protection and safety. It humbles me to know that Your Son prayed the same for me. But I am afraid I have misinterpreted His intent.

I still ask that You would protect me from hurtful things in this world. Yet, even more, I ask that You would protect my soul from the snares of the enemy.

Today, I am facing . . .

In these circumstances, protect me from falling prey to the traps of . . .

Thank You for this eternity-minded protection, which is superior to any temporal protection from harm in this earthly life.

CHAPTER 19

KEEP
THEM SAFE

Tend Your sick ones, O Lord Christ.
Rest Your weary ones, bless Your dying ones,
soothe Your suffering ones, pity Your afflicted ones,
shield Your joyous ones, and all for Your love's sake. Amen.

—AUGUSTINE[1]

*S*everal weeks ago, as I was reading through the seventeenth chapter of John for the umpteenth time, I began to weep inexplicably. As I examined my emotions, I realized that the same portions of the prayer that we highlighted in the last chapter were the ones that were bringing heightened emotion to me on that day.

> Holy Father, protect them by the power of your name (11b).
> While I was with them, I protected them and kept them safe by that name you gave me (12a).
> My prayer is not that you take them out of the world but that you protect from the evil one (15).

Then it dawned on me that my emotions were really responding to the passion expressed by our Savior in this prayer, spoken on the night when He was betrayed into the hands of sinners. Overarching all He said and did with and for His disciples that night was the emotion that expresses His reason for being in that circumstance in the first place: love. God-love. In the Greek, it is *agape.* More than friendship love. More than spousal love. This is a passion for fellowship, an adoration that can be felt only by the Creator for those whom He has created. This is love, that He laid down His life for His beloved. Not only that, but before He did, He carried His beloved before His Father's throne, seeing that they would not suffer loss in His absence. He saw to their care and protection before He would leave them to the devices of a world that hated them (v.14), a world that wished them only evil, a world ruled by the enemy of their souls.

Early in His ministry He had explained this love to the religious ruler Nicodemus in the now-famous passage recorded in John 3: "For God loved the world so much that he gave his only Son so that anyone who believes in him shall not perish but have eternal life" (v. 16 TLB).

God loved the world *so* much.

I can remember playing a childhood game with my parents at bedtime. I'd hold my arms a few inches apart and say, "Do you love me this much?" My parents would nod. Then I'd spread my arms farther apart and ask the question again. Again they would respond in the affirmative. Finally, I would spread my arms as wide as I could and ask, "Do you love me to infinity?" Of course, they told me they did.

We don't need to play this childish game with our heavenly Father. When His Son's arms were spread wide on the cross, He showed that He loves us to infinity and more besides. It is a love that Christ expressed verbally in His high priestly prayer. "May they also be in us" (John 17:21); "I want those you have given me to be with me where I am" (v. 24); "that the love you have for me may be in them and that I myself may be in them" (v. 26). Are you sensing the love—the passion—the heartfelt concern for the safety of His beloved?

These are emotions we can share, at least partially, with Jesus.

We, too, have loved ones, people for whose best interests we would sacrifice ourselves. They may be children or a spouse, parents, siblings, or special friends. Regardless, we recognize that our ability to protect them is insufficient. They need more security than we, as mortal beings, can offer. So, as Jesus did on that dark night of His own soul, we can bring our loved ones to the Father's throne and entrust them to the only One who is able to keep them from the grasp of the Evil One in this world. As Jesus interceded for us, His loved ones, so we can intercede for our loved ones.

How did Jesus intercede for us in love? First, He was bold to express exactly what He desired for us: "I want those you have given me to be with me where I am" (John 17:24). There. He said it. Submitting, of course, to the Father's will, Jesus expressed His ultimate desire for us. Modeling our prayers after His example, then, we can come boldly to God's throne (in Jesus' name) and plainly ask God for their salvation, for their eternal souls. There is no expression of love greater than that which seeks the best interests of the beloved. And certainly an eternity in heaven is in their best interests.

Note, second, that Jesus was careful not to ask for easy lives for us ("My prayer is not that you take them out of the world." [v. 15]); instead He requested the knowledge of God's ever-present hand guiding, directing, leading, and protecting. It is easy for us to pray that those we love would have cushy lives, unchallenged by difficult choices, unmarred by pain and sorrow. What would Jesus say to those prayers? Listen to the words that lead into John 17: "I have told you these things, so that in me you may have peace. In this world you will have trouble. But take heart! I have overcome the world" (16:33). We would not be praying according to His will if we requested a life of unchallenged ease for our loved ones. Instead, we must ask that God will keep them out of the grasp of evil, at peace and trusting Him in the midst of difficulties.

Finally, Jesus prays for our relationship with Him and His Father. "I in them and you in me" so they may know that You "have loved them even as you have loved me" (17:23). We, too, can pray not only that our loved ones will have strong, vibrant relationships here on this earth, but more important, that their relationship with the Father will grow and mature with a oneness that yields much profit for God's kingdom.

Yes, we will continue to pray for skinned knees, lost eyeglasses, runny noses, and safe travels for our loved ones, because those things do concern us in this world. But let's not exclude the life-changing issues of their salvation, their spiritual maturity, their trust in our Lord in every circumstance of life. The answers to these prayers have ramifications that are nothing short of eternal.

PERSONAL PRAYER STARTER

Loving Father,

Following Jesus' example, I carry before You today these individuals whom I love dearly . . .

Please protect them from the hurts and pains of life. But more important I pray for their spiritual growth and relationship with You. I pray that . . .

Thank You for the love You displayed for us, and for the love You have given me for these my family and friends.

NOTE

1. Augustine, bishop of Hippo, quoted in Ken Gire, comp. and ed., *Between Heaven and Earth: Prayers and Reflections That Celebrate an Intimate God* (San Francisco: HarperSanFrancisco, 1997), 97.

CHAPTER 20

SHIELD ME FROM THE TEMPTER

What a Friend we have in Jesus,
All our sins and griefs to bear!
What a privilege to carry
Everything to God in prayer!

—JOSEPH SCRIVEN (1819–86), "WHAT A FRIEND WE HAVE IN JESUS"

*H*is name was Joseph Scriven. Born in 1819, he graduated from Trinity College, Dublin, Ireland, in 1842. In 1843, on the night before his wedding, his fiancée drowned. Years later, in England, Joseph's new girlfriend spurned his interest to marry another man. After moving to Canada and supporting himself as a tutor, Joseph met Catherine Roche, a niece to the woman whose children he tutored. They were engaged. As the two became more attached, Catherine was converted to the faith and baptized by immersion in Rice Lake in 1860. Chilled in the cold water, Catherine developed pneumonia and died before the two could be married. Twenty-six years later, Joseph's dying wish was to be buried next to his beloved Catherine.

Scriven processed his grief with pen in hand. And, although the date of the writing of his best-remembered poem is unknown, this man whose life was marked by bitter tragedy from beginning to end wrote the words to the comforting and beloved hymn "What a Friend We Have in Jesus," still a favorite more than a century after his death.

Listen closely to the emotion, the problem, and the solution Scriven posed in that hymn's second verse:

> *Have we trials and temptations?*
> *Is there trouble anywhere?*
> *We should never be discouraged;*
> *Take it to the Lord in prayer.*
>
> *Can we find a friend so faithful*
> *Who will all our sorrows share?*
> *Jesus knows our every weakness;*
> *Take it to the Lord in prayer.*

Few novelists would be so bold as to try their readers' patience with the bitter twists of fate that mark the real-life story of Joseph Scriven. Few fiction aficionados would be so naive as to believe that waters could claim both of Scriven's fiancées, that his life would be marked with episodes of unrequited love, and that a beloved hero would go to his grave never having married.

And yet, these are the trials and temptations our Lord chose for His servant Joseph Scriven. Having embraced these experiences, Scriven knew that his comfort would only come when he carried all of his burdens to his Best Friend in prayer. Armed with the real-life application of that knowledge, Scriven spent the rest of his days introducing people to Jesus, seeing to their physical needs (as much as was in his power), praying for the sick, and comforting the downtrodden.[1]

What of our own trials and temptations? What of the traps the Evil One places in our own paths? Do the episodes of trauma that mar our lives cause us to slink back into the shadows of God's kingdom work, or do they lead us to a deeper commitment to do our Father's work, as they did for Joseph Scriven?

Remember Jesus' words, "In the world you will have tribulation; but be of good cheer, I have overcome the world" (John 16:33 NKJV). Supplement that knowledge with the words penned by one of Jesus' listeners, the apostle Peter: "So then, those who suffer according to God's will should commit themselves to their faithful Creator and continue to do good" (1 Peter 4:19).

Those Scriptures capsulize Scriven's life.

It is true that in our own strength, our ability to process this kind of grief and to go on serving Christ is sadly inadequate. However, Jesus invites us to take heart, to lean on Him, because He has carried all our griefs, all our temptations, all our sorrows on His shoulders. The writer to the Hebrews explains, "For we do not have a high priest who is unable to sympathize with our weaknesses, but we have one who has been tempted in every way, just as we are—yet was without sin. Let us then approach the throne of grace with confidence, so that we may receive mercy and find grace to help us in our time of need" (4:15–16).

When Jesus taught His disciples to pray, one of the key elements was this request: "Lead us not into temptation, but deliver us from the evil one" (Matthew 6:13). Intriguingly a similar phrase appears in Jesus' prayer for us in John 17: "Protect them from the evil one" (v. 15). His protection comes in many forms; one of the greatest is described in depth in the latter half of Ephesians 6, where Paul tells of our need for God's armor and the results that come of dressing in that armor on a daily basis. His challenge to us is: "Therefore put on the full armor of God, so that when the day of evil comes, you may be able to stand your ground, and after you have done everything, to stand" (v. 13).

Remembering that the enemy prowls around like a hungry lion interested only in devouring us so we will be unable to fulfill God's purposes (1 Peter 5:8), our prayer pattern should be that described in Scriven's hymn. Whenever we encounter temptations, we must waste no time in packaging them up and carrying them before our Lord in prayer. Acknowledging our inability to combat temptation on our own, we can approach God's throne of grace with the request that He would equip us with all the battle resources we need to withstand the snares evil has placed in our path. He is pleased with our request that when the battle is over, we will be left standing, our feet planted more firmly than ever on the solid ground of our faith in Jesus Christ and His ability to overcome evil.

PERSONAL PRAYER STARTER

———— ✑ ————

Powerful Father,

After reading about the trials of your servant Joseph Scriven, I have a different perspective on my own difficult circumstances. After thinking about Scriven's challenge for me to carry everything to You in prayer, I want to submit to You these trying elements of my life . . .

As I face these temptations today, please equip me with . . .

that in the end I may be found standing in awe before Your throne.

———— ✑ ————

NOTE

1. Background on Scriven obtained from Foster Meharry Russell, *What a Friend We Have in Jesus* (Belleville, Ontario: Mika, 1981).

CHAPTER 21

∽

FOCUSED ON GOD'S PRIORITIES

∽

I'm single-minded in pursuit of you;
don't let me miss the road signs you've posted.
I've banked your promises in the vault of my heart
so I won't sin myself bankrupt.

—PSALM 119:10 THE MESSAGE

I'd like you to meet Ruby Eliason. I'd like you to, but you can't. Ruby died last spring. It's a shame, though. You'd have liked her. And respected her. Everyone did. She was a doer. Proactive. Forward-looking.

By the world's standards, Ruby didn't amount to much. She didn't marry, nor did she bear children. She didn't accumulate money, position, or power. But then those never were her intent. She did travel the world, living abroad in India and Africa.

Ruby was a nurse. A nurse with two master's degrees and a Ph.D. in health development—a Ph.D. earned in her retirement, so she could stay active and useful at work as a missionary among villagers in Cameroon, Africa, long after most other seniors would have hung up their white uniforms and retired to Florida's palm-lined beaches. But not Ruby. And not her colleague, medical doctor Laura Edwards.

Together the two spent up to seven months each year of their retirement on the mission field in Cameroon, where Ruby had worked as a career missionary. They trained birth attendants and helped prepare women from forty remote villages to administer immunizations, medications, and sanitation standards. And all the while, they led villagers to Christ and discipled them in His ways. Being living examples of godliness seemed to come as naturally as breathing to the two.

Once, I asked Ruby what she had given up for the sake of God's call. I asked whether she had any regrets. She answered, "It has been no sacrifice. It has been a great privilege. My work is so enriching. God has given me health and preparation for continuing ministry. So, why not do it?"

Ruby and Laura were on the field again this spring, en route to a remote village, when the steering mechanism on their vehicle broke, throwing both women from the vehicle as it careened over a cliff. In a split second they died on the ground where they had given their lives away piece by piece, with a single-minded focus that bespeaks their wholehearted commitment to growing God's kingdom.

Several times in John 17 Jesus prayed that we would be unified, even as He, the Father, and the Holy Spirit are unified—of one mind and purpose. This prayer has so many nuances, so many rich meanings, that it will take an examination from several perspectives for us to fully appreciate it. Today, though, we can look to Ruby's and Laura's example as we examine an oft-overlooked aspect of Jesus' prayer for our oneness; that is, a unified focus or a single-mindedness within our own hearts. It is a prayer we must echo daily if we are to please our Master.

Here's a principle of God's kingdom: If we give our lives away for those things that are important to Him, if we focus on His concerns, He will take care of those things that concern us. Our loved ones. Our careers. Our homes and our finances. This is consistent with Jesus' words,

> Therefore I tell you, do not worry about your life, what you will eat or drink; or about your body, what you will wear. Is not life more important than food, and the body more important than clothes? . . . For the pagans run after all these things, and your heavenly Father knows that you need them. But seek first his kingdom and his righteousness, and all these things will be given to you as well. (Matthew 6:25, 32–33)

Seek first His kingdom's interests. Make the most of every opportunity for service. Use all of our God-given resources toward kingdom purposes—our time, our energies, our earning power. And we will be compensated accordingly—in the things of value to God's kingdom, not necessarily in the things of value to this temporary world where cars rust, houses decay, clothes become frayed and tattered, and loved ones die.

A good supervisor looks out for the best interests of his workers. He compensates them well, gives them needed rest times, encourages them when they are discouraged. If an earthly supervisor does that for his employees, how much more will our Master who loves us look after all of our needs, as we work faithfully for Him?

Will every one of us be called to career mission service in the remote regions of India or Africa? No. But each of us must follow Christ without looking back to those things we have left behind—those earthly pleasures we think we are missing because we are following the path the Master has set out for us.

Listen to Jesus' hard response to the man who wanted to say good-bye to his family before following Christ: "No one who puts his hand to the plow and looks back is fit for service in the kingdom of God" (Luke 9:62). According to the *Explorer's Bible Study* commentary, "To look back would be to make a crooked furrow or a crooked row. You have to keep your eye upon the mark and be single-minded in your purpose."[1]

Think of Ruby's words: "It has been no sacrifice. It has been a great privilege." I believe therein lies the key to our unity of purpose: If we look at life with Christ as a series of sacrifices (saying, "I can't do that, because I'm a Christian"), we will be divided in purpose, plowing a crooked furrow, because our eyes will be constantly looking over our shoulders to the fun experiences other people get to have while we are too busy working to engage in enjoyable activities. If, instead, we see our walk with Christ as a daily adventure, a privilege of being chosen to work with His purposes, we will be content, even excited to do our best work, to give our best efforts toward plowing in His field—wherever He has called us to serve.

PERSONAL PRAYER STARTER

Master of the fields,
    You know I have looked back at all I've given up to serve You.
But seeing the example of Ruby's and Laura's wholehearted service to You, I am convicted of my double-mindedness.
    God, I entrust to You those things I have left behind . . .
    Help me focus only on those things You have set before me to do. Those are . . .
    I choose to serve You with wholehearted abandon, wherever You place me.

NOTE

1. *Explorer's Bible Study: Luke and Acts, Workbook,* electronic ed. Copyright © 1978, 1988 N. E. Constance.

PART FOUR

God's INTERESTS FOR US

*Only God knows what is ultimately
in our best interest, but Jesus' prayer
gives us a glimpse of some of the areas
in which He desires to bless us.*

c০

RECOGNIZING HIS CALL

c০

*Sweetest Lord, make me appreciative of the dignity of my high
vocation, and its many responsibilities. Never permit me
to disgrace it by giving way to coldness, unkindness, or impatience.*

—MOTHER TERESA[1]

I remember how my mom used to call me when I was a child. I'd
be playing noisily in a neighbor's backyard with a crowd of friends
when the chime of my great-grandmother's antique school bell
would ring through the yard—a distinctive and conspicuous sound,
even several houses down the street. My mom didn't believe in
counting to three, like modern mothers do. ("I'm warning you, if I
count to three and you're not here, I'll . . .") When my mom called,
it was my responsibility to double-time it back home. A second call
would result in punishment—which it is in my nature to avoid. So
I'd listen for the bell, dropping everything to follow its peals to my
own back door.

As God's daughters and sons, all of us have responded to the
clarion call of God. His first bell called us to Jesus' cross, where we
found mercy and forgiveness. Remember, we did not initiate our
own salvation. Rather, God's Spirit drew us to that cross, softened

our hearts, opened our minds to understand the simple message of the gospel, and even made us willing to admit our faults in order to obtain forgiveness. The Holy Spirit attuned us to the unique frequency of the bell, teaching us to recognize and respond to it.

The call of God didn't end with us tumbling safely just inside the borders of His kingdom, however. Once we were inside the boundaries, He issued a call that requires us to "live a life worthy of the calling." To "be completely humble and gentle; be patient, bearing with one another in love" (Ephesians 4:1–2). To live a holy life, in accordance with God's purpose for us (2 Timothy 1:9).

The special plan He created you and me to fulfill is the subject of the specific calls He places upon our lives. If only His calls were as physically audible as my mother's bell. But His calls originate in the invisible world, are confirmed by Scripture, and are designed to make the best use of the talents He endowed on each of us.

Your call from God and mine are similar in that they are consistent with Jesus' commission to "go and make disciples of all nations." Yet our calls may be different from that of a friend who is a graphic artist, a career missionary in Cameroon, or a medical doctor practicing at the Mayo Clinic.

According to Paul, "God's gifts and his call are irrevocable" (Romans 11:29). His call stands, even when we are slow to respond. Patiently, He rings the bell over and over until we choose (of our own accord) to run home, to heed the call.

I wish I could give you a receiver tuned to God's calling frequency. But I can't tell you how God will issue His call for you. Isaiah and Ezekiel saw God on His throne; Moses heard His voice from a burning bush. But seldom does God work through such obvious means these days. In our day God usually speaks through our prayerful consideration of His written Word. Let me assure you that as you prayerfully seek His call, you will find it. Jesus said, "My sheep hear My voice, and I know them, and they follow Me" (John 10:27 NKJV). Keep knocking on heaven's door; persist in your prayers for a clear understanding of His calling. You won't be disappointed.

Once we do know God's purpose for our lives, there is a temptation to measure our purpose against the purposes God has for other believers. Lest we become haughty about the relative merits of our own calling, Paul reminds us, "Think of what you were when you were called. Not many of you were wise by human standards; not many were influential; not many were of noble birth. But God chose the foolish things of the world to shame the wise . . . so that no one may boast before him" (1 Corinthians 1:26–27, 29).

Whatever orders God has signed for our lives, we each must determine how to respond. In the 1970s I heard the story of Arthur Blessed, who prayed as a new believer that God would give everyone else the good jobs that required class and finesse. Instead, Arthur asked for the privilege of being God's garbage man, the one who would do the dirty jobs no one else wanted, just for the privilege of serving the One who saved him. Arthur responded to God's call with an earnestness that would shame most of us. You are mistaken if you think God won't use a person who responds likewise to His call.

This acknowledgment of God's call will bring us, eventually, to the point Jesus reached when He told His Father, "I brought glory to you here on earth by doing everything you told me to do" (John 17:4 NLT).

All through the Gospels we read that Jesus went alone to pray to His Father. He did so before choosing His disciples (Luke 6), on the Mount of Transfiguration (Luke 9), before He walked on the water and saved His disciples from a powerful storm (Matthew 14), and of course in the Garden of Gethsemane before taking that long, lonely walk down the Via Dolorosa to Calvary (Matthew 26). It was through prayer that He knew He had accomplished the Father's will each day. Not only did He hear the call, seeking regular direction by making time alone with the Father, but once the direction was clear, Jesus did everything the Father set before Him to do. Let's go and do likewise.

PERSONAL PRAYER STARTER
———————— ✑ ————————

My Lord and Master,

I am humbled to know that, unworthy though I am, You have a calling, a purpose just for me to fulfill.

I am eager to learn everything I can about Your call on my life. I know You have gifted me in the areas of . . . Would You show me exactly what calling, what purpose You have for me?

I understand that You desire of all believers that we live a life worthy of the calling. Help me to do this in the areas of . . .

And, Master, I thank You for this valued calling.

———————— ✑ ————————

NOTE

1. Mother Teresa of Calcutta, quoted in Ken Gire, comp. and ed., *Between Heaven and Earth: Prayers and Reflections That Celebrate an Intimate God* (San Francisco: HarperSanFrancisco, 1997).

CHAPTER 23

WHAT'S ALL THIS ABOUT FRUIT?

Down in the human heart, Crushed by the tempter,
Feelings lie buried that grace can restore;
Touched by a loving heart, Wakened by kindness,
Chords that were broken will vibrate once more.
—FANNY J. CROSBY (1820–1915), "RESCUE THE PERISHING"

There is nothing as tedious as a repetitive job, one whose ultimate value we don't see. Manufacturers have found that if an individual's job is to turn the same bolt in the same type of part passing by on an assembly line hour after hour, he will be more content (and less apt to be careless in his bolt turning) if he is reminded how important that bolt is to the finished vehicle, appliance, or device.

Value. We all want to do something of value. Something that matters. Something that has the ability to transcend our own little worlds.

Every human has an innate desire to feel useful and productive, to feel that one's life matters. We avoid tedious, repetitive tasks because in doing them we feel like drones, less human, more mechanical. And yet, someone must be willing to subject herself to these tasks, for they must be done.

We all could name some tedious but necessary jobs. How can

you and I approach these jobs with the attitude Arthur Blessed displayed? We can be willing to work in the trash heaps as long as it benefits God's kingdom, willing to find value in dirty work.

Tedium is in the eye of the worker. Some moms might find two years of changing dirty diapers tedious, whereas others see it as a loving act of service to a little person who has intrinsic value. Those mothers might pray over their children during diaper time, sing to them, tickle them, hug them tight. Similarly, some people flying across the country might find the flight time a necessary evil to be endured hidden behind a folded newspaper page or paperback book, whereas others might use the opportunity to build a relationship with a fellow passenger who seems to want to talk—expressing genuine interest in their days' challenges, maybe even earning a hearing for the message of Christ.

The latter approaches lead to using even "throwaway" time in ways that have eternal value. They transform a profitless attitude of tedium into a mind-set that allows for usefulness and productivity. As believers in Christ we have opportunities every day to affect the eternal destinies of those we meet. We can lead others to Christ, we can equip fellow believers, we can offer service to Christ that will build for us a treasure cache in heaven.

The New Testament has a term for that approach to life; it's called "bearing fruit." *Vine's Expository Dictionary of Biblical Words* explains the Bible's fruit metaphors:

> Fruit [is] the visible expression of power working inwardly and invisibly, the character of the fruit [is] evidence of the character of the power producing it. As the visible expressions of hidden lusts are the works of the flesh, so the invisible power of the Holy Spirit in those who are brought into living union with Christ produces "the fruit of the Spirit."[1]

It is an apt description. Outside my office window my father planted apple trees years ago. Day after day these trees stand in the same place, processing the same nutrients to produce the same variety of fruit. To some, it would seem tedious, repetitive; and yet, these trees are fruitful. Each apple contains seeds that allow it to reproduce itself. The trees can trace their heritage to the seeds of older trees, in an unbroken chain of fruitfulness that leads back to the original apple tree God created at the beginning of time.

You and I are not just the fruit of Jesus' ministry, but that of His disciples. Just like my family's apple trees, we can trace our spiritual heritage in an unbroken line of fruitfulness of believers telling the gospel, nurturing new believers, and training others in the ways of Christ that leads all the way back to New Testament times. "My prayer is not for [these disciples] alone. I pray also for those who will believe in me through their message," Jesus said in John 17:20. He prayed for the fruit of His followers' faithful service. He prayed for the fruit of your service and mine. For it is our responsibility to continue that chain, unbroken.

By speaking these words on our behalf, Jesus showed that God is not just interested in our hearing His call; rather, He is concerned with the fruits our lives exhibit. Because the fruits on the outside are an indication of what's going on inside our hearts and minds—as Vine's dictionary explained, our variety of fruit is a reflection of the power at work within. "For the mouth speaks out of that which fills the heart," Jesus told His listeners (Matthew 12:34 NASB).

Introducing the fruit analogy (one of His more frequently used metaphors) Jesus told another crowd, "Every good tree bears good fruit, but a bad tree bears bad fruit" (Matthew 7:17). He explained further to His followers, "This is to my Father's glory, that you bear much fruit, showing yourselves to be my disciples" (John 15:8). So, if the Spirit of God truly lives within me, He will make me a bearer of good fruit. If I'm not bearing good fruit, perhaps I'm not allowing God's Spirit to rule in my heart, as He ought.

Let's make this interest God holds for us a matter of prayer today, before we examine the specific fruit God's Spirit will equip us to bear.

PERSONAL PRAYER STARTER

———————— ✑ ————————

Master of the vineyard,

I am afraid that the bitter fruit that I bear at times is an indication of a greater problem—I am not allowing Your Spirit to control every aspect of my life. I have been holding on to the areas of . . . I surrender these, now, to You.

Sometimes my perspective is all wrong. I look at those things You have set before me to do as tedious, beneath me, rather than seeing them as opportunities for fruitful service to You. Please equip me to change my approach and my attitude as I face these tasks today . . .

———————— ✑ ————————

NOTE

1. *Vine's Expository Dictionary of Biblical Words*, electronic ed. (Nashville: Nelson, 1997), s.v. "Fruit (Bear), Fruitful, Unfruitful."

CHAPTER 24

CLOSE-UPS OF GOOD FRUIT

*Many love Jesus as long as they meet with no adversity,
many praise Him and bless Him as long as they receive
some consolations from Him.*

—THOMAS À KEMPIS[1]

*N*ow that we have again settled the issue of living a life controlled by God's Spirit (have you noticed that we must revisit this issue periodically, as the temptation is great to retake the captain's chair for ourselves?), we are ready to take a closer look at the good fruit God's Spirit will produce in us.

Of the many texts in Paul's epistles that challenge us to bear the fruit of godliness, the most complete explanation comes in his letter to the Galatian believers, when he writes, "But the fruit of the Spirit is love, joy, peace, patience, kindness, goodness, faithfulness, gentleness and self-control. Against such things there is no law" (5:22–23).

A little background on the situation that prompted Paul's writing to the Galatians would be in order. According to *Nelson's Illustrated Bible Dictionary,* in Galatians Paul "forcefully proclaims the doctrine of justification by faith alone. . . . The peals of its liberating truth have thundered down through the centuries, calling men and women to new life by the grace of God."[2]

Why was it necessary for Paul to remind these believers of this eternal truth? After Paul left Galatia, false religious leaders had convinced Galatian Christians that the gospel Paul had taught was not enough.

It is always meaningful for us, as we study Scripture, to grasp the historical context in which it was written. In this case, it is invaluable to know that the discussion of the fruit God's Spirit produces in our lives comes after the declaration that we can't produce these good works ourselves. Our salvation and our changed lives are a result of our faith in God's power to save and change us. They cannot be contrived by any actions we take of our own accord.

The fruit God's Spirit produces is an exhibit of the highest qualities human nature was designed to display—before sin entered the picture. Let's hear the list again: "love, joy, peace, patience, kindness, goodness, faithfulness, gentleness and self-control."

In the Spirit-controlled believer these are the outgrowths of what is going on inside. The goodness is not feigned. The kindness is not hiding a selfish ulterior motive. The self-control does not serve as a thin screen to a seething cauldron of bitterness. The outward peace does not mask an inner eruption of molten turmoil. The joy is not a shallow, happy-all-the-time, head-in-the-sand approach to life.

Rather, the love is an expression of the unconditional *agape* God-love He has lavished upon us. The joy is a sense of contentment, a resting in that Father-love, depending upon that love to do the best for us. The peace is an inner calm in the midst of difficult circumstances—based upon the assurance that ultimate victory comes for the believer in the next life, if not always in this one.

The patience is a willingness to wait for God's plan to unfold, rather than succumbing to the temptation to force things to happen on our timetable. The kindness is the outcropping of an inner desire to see that others are well taken care of, a genuine desire to value others, even if that means they get ahead of us in the trappings of this world.

The goodness is a reflection of that character trait of God. We've all heard a preacher announce, "God is good," to which the congregation responds, "All the time." "All the time," says the preacher. "God is good," responds the congregation. Does that mean I will always understand His ways? Certainly not. But God's goodness does not vary depending upon the things He allows to touch my life. God is good *all* the time. And so must I be. Good to others when they are not good to me. Seeking their best when they ignore me or wish evil on me. Remember, when Jesus prayed, He acknowledged the fact that the world would not only misunderstand, but even hate us. Because we are citizens of another world, we don't belong here any more than He did (John 17:14). So, no matter how our goodness is received, we must continue to offer it without reservation.

The faithfulness speaks of our fidelity, our trustworthiness. According to Bible commentator Adam Clarke, faithfulness means "conscientious carefulness in preserving what is committed to our trust . . . neither betraying the secret of our friend, nor disappointing the confidence of our employer."[3] That definition hits where we live. In keeping confidences, in operating with integrity in employment and friendship situations, in restraining the temptation to cheat or to gossip. A whole book's worth of truth resides in that little Greek word, *pistis,* which translates as "faithfulness."

Then there's gentleness. Clarke calls the fruit of gentleness a "rare grace." It is more than polished manners, because again the gentleness flows from a graceful inner life, a genuine caring for others exhibited in compassionate actions.

Finally, we hear of the fruit of self-control, which is rather a misnomer. It is really God-control. Anyone who has ever tried to stop smoking, cut down on overeating, give up caffeine, or stop at just one Hershey's chocolate kiss knows we don't have enough self-control in ourselves to effect major life changes. But when we allow God to control our lives, trying to control ourselves is no longer an issue.

Which brings us full circle. When God is in control, He will work from inside out to produce in us good fruit, worthy of His good character. And He will do so, all the more, when our prayers reflect our heartfelt desires to be fruitful.

PERSONAL PRAYER STARTER

——————— ✑ ———————

Tender of the fruit,
  After studying the list of fruit Your Spirit exhibits in believers, I
see myself particularly lacking in the area of . . .
  Would You work on that area for me this week? Would You
help me exhibit that quality, even when I am in the situations of . . .
  I thank You that while You call me to bear good fruit, You
equip me to do so.

——————— ✑ ———————

NOTES

1. Thomas à Kempis (1379–1471), from *Imitatio Christi (The Imitation of Christ)*, as collected in *2000 Years Since Bethlehem: Images of Christ Through the Centuries*, compiled by Janice T. Grana (Nashville: Upper Room Books, 1998).

2. *Nelson's Illustrated Bible Dictionary*, electronic ed. (Nashville: Nelson, 1986), s.v. "Galatians, Epistle to the."

3. *Adam Clarke Commentary*, electronic ed., s.v. "Galatians 5:22."

CHAPTER 25

IT'S WHY HE GAVE US EARS

For the words which You gave Me I have given to them;
and they received them and truly understood that
I came forth from You, and they believed that You sent Me.
—JOHN 17:8 NASB

*I*t's a complaint countless women voice to their husbands: "You're not *listening* to me." Although husbands and wives may hear each other's words, they are not always equipped to listen. After all our sensitivity training and political correctness indoctrination, there continues to be a shortage of listening. Everyone's talking. Everyone demands to be heard. But few truly hear.

The ancient Hebrew language had a word for listening: *shama*. It was used more than 1,100 times in the Old Testament. Throughout the wisdom literature. The history books. The prophetic books. And in New Testament Greek, no fewer than seven verbs express nuances of the concept of hearing and listening. It seems listening was a high priority with God, and humans needed frequent reminders to listen to Him.

Many of the uses of the Hebrew word *shama* come in the prophetic books, where the Almighty pleads with His people to "listen" to Him, to "hear" His words; where He chides them in the harshest tones for failing to listen and understand His ways. Over and over He pleads, "Listen to Me." And it seems that few other than His own prophets heeded His words. (See Isaiah 44, 46, and 48, and Ezekiel 33:30–33 for a few examples.)

Listen to Jesus' lament, echoing the prophet Isaiah's words,

> You will hear my words, but you will not understand; you will see what I do, but you will not perceive its meaning. For the hearts of these people are hardened, and their ears cannot hear, and they have closed their eyes—so their eyes cannot see, and their ears cannot hear, and their hearts cannot understand. (Matthew 13:14–15 NLT)

However, Jesus continued, "But blessed are your eyes, because they see; and your ears, because they hear" (Matthew 13:16 NLT). So He equipped His followers with the ability to receive God's words, to hear from heaven. He placed within us a longing for that interaction. And He handed over to His followers all the words the Father wanted them to have. "For the words which You gave Me I have given to them; and they received them," He said (John 17:8 NASB).

But are we still receiving those words today? Are we still equipped to hear from heaven? Or have we lost our attentiveness to the sound of His voice?

We approach communication with God bearing a long list of requests. Now that we're nearly halfway through our study of Jesus' high priestly prayer, perhaps our request list has become more God-honoring, more attuned to His desires for us. However, while listing our requests, we seldom leave time for silence before God's throne. Instead, we babble on and on, like adolescents thinking our many words will make us sound wiser, droning on until we feel we have covered all possible topics several times over, fearing even the occasional silent moment as if we were broadcasting on a radio station where pauses are expressly forbidden.

When we talked about recognizing the call God placed on our lives, we briefly addressed the idea that God has something to say to us. Sometimes it is direction. Other times it is an expression of loving care, an encouragement to stay the course, or a prick of conscience to correct us when we sin. Perhaps He will bring a Scripture promise to mind, cause us to remember a principle from our pastor's sermon, or make alive a passage we've just read. In my life, He often works through the lyrics of biblically based hymns and songs, because their tunes echo down the passageways of my mind and draw out areas where my life is inconsistent with Scripture.

"For the word of God is living and active. Sharper than any double-edged sword, it penetrates even to dividing soul and spirit, joints and marrow; it judges the thoughts and attitudes of the heart" (Hebrews 4:12). God's active, living Word speaks volumes to us today, even though it has been nearly two millennia since its last words were penned. God still speaks, but our own many words can drown out His still, small voice. Remember how God showed Himself to Elijah in 1 Kings 19:11–13:

> The Lord said, "Go out and stand on the mountain in the presence of the Lord, for the Lord is about to pass by." Then a great and powerful wind tore the mountains apart and shattered the rocks before the Lord, but the Lord was not in the wind. After the wind there was an earthquake, but the Lord was not in the earthquake. After the earthquake came a fire, but the Lord was not in the fire. And after the fire came a gentle whisper. When Elijah heard it, he pulled his cloak over his face and went out and stood at the mouth of the cave.

God spoke to Elijah, not in the cacophony of powerful noise, but in the stillness of a gentle whisper. The Holy Spirit, the God-sent counselor who reminds us of the things Jesus taught about His Father, is gentle in His dealings with us. He does not demand to be heard above the noise of our lives. Rather, He speaks softly, persistently, offering God's insight to those who have ears and are willing to listen. To those who have eyes that are ready to see. To those who will sit in silence until all the sounds of this world die down, leaving only the recognizable voice of the Master, the One who called out for Adam and Eve in the Garden of Eden in the cool of the day, "Where are you?" (Genesis 3:9).

Hear the words of the resurrected Jesus to the church of Laodicea: "Here I am! I stand at the door and knock. If anyone hears my voice and opens the door, I will come in and eat with him, and he with me" (Revelation 3:20).

What God wants from our prayer life is the two-way relationship Jesus modeled; both parties listened and both parties spoke. We have a God who wants to hear from us, and we have a God who wants to speak to us. The question is: Can we discipline ourselves to remain silent long enough to listen? Or will He continue to issue the call, "Where are you? Please listen to Me!"

PERSONAL PRAYER STARTER

Patient Father,

Today, I hold back all my requests. You know the list. We've been down it together many times.

Rather, I offer these moments of silence to You. I want to listen. Attune me to Your voice. Speak to me; I want to hear . . .

CHAPTER 26

ငၵာ

THE CHOICE
TO OBEY

ငၵာ

Finish then Thy new creation,
Pure and spotless let us be;
Let us see Thy great salvation
Perfectly restored in Thee.
—CHARLES WESLEY (1707–88), "LOVE DIVINE ALL LOVES EXCELLING"

*I*nseparable from the issue of listening to God's voice is the inherent demand that once we hear, we must obey—willingly and with sold-out effort.

According to *Nelson's Illustrated Bible Dictionary,* "In both the Old and New Testaments the word *obey* is related to the idea of hearing. Obedience is a positive, active response to what a person hears."[1] To listen. To attend to what we hear. To submit. To obey. These are all components to the prayer where we are still before our Master, listening only for His clear, distinct voice.

God presented the Israelites with a clear choice: Obey and be blessed; disobey and be cursed. He didn't deviate from swift execution of this choice's consequences. Disobedient Israelites were alternately swallowed by an earthquake, stricken with leprosy, given over into captivity, and punished with famine. Obedient Israelites watched God fight battle after battle for them; they followed a visible representation of His presence through the wilderness; they filled their stomachs with mysterious manna; they lived in safety, protected from their enemies. It would seem, though, that the living out of obedience was against the grain of human nature, even for God's chosen people who had seen the clear evidence of His pleasure and His displeasure played out with equal alacrity.

In the New Testament, while the punishment is not as quick or readily apparent, the requirements of obedience are no less stringent: "We know that we have come to know him if we obey his commands. The man who says, 'I know him,' but does not do what he commands is a liar." These are strong words from John the beloved (1 John 2:3–4).

Echoing this truth, Paul makes a strong statement that we would do well to memorize and to emulate: "We demolish arguments and every pretension that sets itself up against the knowledge of God, and we take captive every thought to make it obedient to Christ" (2 Corinthians 10:5). This word picture conjures in my mind a metal ball attached to a multistory crane that is able to topple a high-rise complex with a few well-placed hits. I find myself wanting to find a spiritual wrecking ball that will demolish all of the resistance to God that has taken up residence in my mind, the swinging ball that will leave standing only my desire to obey, crushing to bits all of my bent toward disobedience.

This demolition plan would please the Master. I know this because in His prayer Jesus commends His followers to the Father for their obedience: "I have revealed you to those whom you gave me out of the world. They were yours; you gave them to me and they have obeyed your word" (John 17:6). According to a statement Jesus made in John 15, our love for Him is what motivates obedience; conversely, those who do not love Him will not (or cannot) obey (vv. 10–12). I do love Him, and I want to love Him even more. But realistically I must acknowledge that I need His help if I am to obey. When I was a child, our church often sang a gospel song titled "Make Me Willing." And that must be my prayer—that I would be willing to obey Him in all circumstances.

I feel comforted that even the apostle Paul had difficulty in this area. He was transparent in his struggle when he told the Roman believers,

> I do not understand what I do. For what I want to do I do not do, but what I hate I do. . . . When I want to do good, evil is right there with me. For in my inner being I delight in God's law; but I see another law at work in the members of my body, waging war against the law of my mind and making me a prisoner of the law of sin at work within my members. (Romans 7:15, 21–23)

I challenge you to read this entire passage. And don't stop until you have rejoiced in the victory Paul expresses: "Therefore, there is now no condemnation for those who are in Christ Jesus, because through Christ Jesus the law of the Spirit of life set me free from the law of sin and death" (Romans 8:1–2).

I'm so glad the love of Christ is a two-way street. No longer are we punished immediately and decisively for our disobedience. We live in a season when God pours out His grace upon those who desire to obey, even if we do not always succeed in our best intentions. Listen to Jesus' comforting words to the church of Philadelphia in Revelation 3:8: "I know you well; you aren't strong, but you have tried to obey and have not denied my Name. Therefore I have opened a door to you that no one can shut" (TLB).

He understands the difficulty we have in learning obedience. He was human, every bit as much as we are, only He did not succumb to the temptation to sin. "Although he was a son, he learned obedience from what he suffered and, once made perfect, he became the source of eternal salvation for all who obey him" (Hebrews 5:8–9).

Scripture gives a clear prescription for how we are to obey. "As obedient children, do not conform to the evil desires you had when you lived in ignorance. But just as he who called you is holy, so be holy in all you do" (1 Peter 1:14–15). We are called to obey the command to keep our minds and actions pure, holy, set apart for

God's service. Like Jesus, we are called to obedience even when it requires suffering. And like the Israelites, we are called to obedience that doesn't question the Master, doesn't try to set ourselves up as wiser than the all-wise Lord, doesn't try to find ways to circumvent His will for our lives.

PERSONAL PRAYER STARTER

―――――― ∽ ――――――

God, my Father,

Without Your power, I find it nearly impossible to obey You. It's not that I don't want to. I love You. And I desire to obey. But like Paul, I find myself doing the opposite of what I want to do.

I have been slow to obey You when Your requirements have called me to . . .

I don't ask You to make it easy, but I do ask that You change my attitude and make me willing to choose Your will over my own. So I make the conscious choice to obey Your will in the areas of . . .

―――――― ∽ ――――――

NOTE

1. *Nelson's Illustrated Bible Dictionary,* electronic ed. (Nashville: Nelson, 1986), s.v. "obedience."

CHAPTER 27

GROWING UP
(IN THE FAITH)

Open my eyes, that I may see
Glimpses of truth Thou hast for me;
Place in my hands the wonderful key
That shall unclasp and set me free.

Silently now I wait for Thee,
Ready, my God, Thy will to see,
Open my eyes, illumine me,
Spirit divine!

—CLARA H. SCOTT (1841–97), "OPEN MY EYES, THAT I MAY SEE"

*W*hen Jesus prayed for those of us who would be in the ensuing generations of believers, He was prophesying that His followers would not always be the fragile, easily dissuaded, frightened cluster they would prove themselves to be later that night when He was arrested. Instead, with the power of the Holy Spirit, they would one day become a mighty army with a convincing testimony of His saving grace. Jesus saw what would be as if it were already in existence; that is why He was able to pray for those of us who would come after. In their current condition, though, the eleven remaining disciples were not likely to persuade anyone to follow them as they followed Christ.

Let's look into the book of Acts, which records the metamorphosis. After Jesus' resurrection and ascension (forty days later), His followers

> returned to Jerusalem from the hill called the Mount of Olives, a Sabbath day's walk from the city. When they arrived, they went upstairs to

the room where they were staying. Those present were Peter, John, James and Andrew; Philip and Thomas, Bartholomew and Matthew; James son of Alphaeus and Simon the Zealot, and Judas son of James. They all joined together constantly in prayer, along with the women and Mary the mother of Jesus, and with his brothers. (Acts 1:12–14)

Did you catch what they did? They prayed. Together. Constantly. Men and women waited for the power Jesus promised to come upon them, to equip them to be His witnesses before the nations. They couldn't know all of the ways God would use them, but they understood enough to realize that they couldn't do it alone. They needed His power. They needed the maturity only He could offer them.

The days after Jesus was taken up into heaven were concentrated times of seeking God. The eventual response from God is that He poured out His power on them, a power that transformed weak, trembling children in the faith into articulate, insightful spiritual giants who won three thousand converts in just one day.

We could debate the meanings of various terms used in Acts 2 and discuss whether God still moves in the same way today. But we won't. Instead let's look at the preparation of the disciples' hearts that allowed God to grow them up. And let's look at how we can prepare our hearts for the growth God wants to bring to us.

When they knew they weren't up for the task ahead, Jesus' followers prayed—with intensity, with persistence. And so must we. But what should we pray?

When Jesus told the parable of the seeds that fell on various soils, He concluded with the seed that fell on good soil, which He defined as "those with a noble and good heart, who hear the word, retain it, and by persevering produce a crop" (Luke 8:15). As this seed took root and grew into a multiplying plant, Jesus said it required a hearing, action, and perseverance—dogged determination and tenacity that clings to the faith even when the winds of the world's false doctrines try to wrench its grip from the rock of salvation. These are requirements of growing tall and strong in the faith, equipped to produce fruit that contains healthy seed.

James built on this foundation when he wrote, "Perseverance must finish its work so that you may be mature and complete, not lacking anything. If any of you lacks wisdom, he should ask God" (James 1:4–5a). In James's mind, then, maturity contains not only an element of perseverance but also an element of wisdom, of discernment, of God-sent insight.

In a similar vein, Paul wrote to the Ephesians, saying that maturity comes when

> we will no longer be infants, tossed back and forth by the waves, and blown here and there by every wind of teaching and by the cunning and craftiness of men in their deceitful scheming. Instead, speaking the truth in love, we will in all things grow up into him who is the Head, that is, Christ. (Ephesians 4:14–15)

Paul adds to our understanding by saying that maturity is in evidence when we know what we believe, when we know the ways of God and the Scriptures so well that even the most cunning scheme cannot dissuade us from what we know to be true.

Now that we understand a bit about the growth the Master expects us to exhibit, Paul's prayer for the Ephesians is perhaps our best pattern as we pray for maturity:

> I pray that from his glorious, unlimited resources he will give you mighty inner strength through his Holy Spirit. And I pray that Christ will be more and more at home in your hearts as you trust in him. May your roots go down deep into the soil of God's marvelous love. And may you have the power to understand, as all God's people should, how wide, how long, how high, and how deep his love really is. May you experience the love of Christ, though it is so great you will never fully understand it. Then you will be filled with the fullness of life and power that comes from God (Ephesians 3:16–19 NLT).

My prayer is that this study will be a step toward that brand of maturity in your life, so that one day together we might be presented to Jesus "as a radiant church, without stain or wrinkle or any other blemish, but holy and blameless" (Ephesians 5:27).

PERSONAL PRAYER STARTER

My Lord,

I am not content to just slide safely past the borders of heaven. I want to grow up, to mature in my knowledge of You. I want to be productive, reproducing the faith You have given me so that others may come to know You as I have.

So I ask that You would grant me the insight I need to face . . .

Also, I ask that You would empower me to persevere in . . .

Finally, please help me experience You in such a way that I am filled up with You . . .

CHAPTER 28

KEEP ON SEEING GOD

O Holy Spirit, As the sun is full of light, the ocean full of water,
Heaven full of glory, so may my heart be full of Thee. . . .
Give me Thyself without measure, as an unimpaired fountain,
as inexhaustible riches.

—PURITAN PRAYER[1]

Twice so far in this study we have undertaken to see a picture of
who God is. First we caught a glimpse of His glory, as described by
Ezekiel, Isaiah, and John. Then we tried to extrapolate from Jesus'
descriptions of His Father what some of His character traits are. The
scope of each chapter of this study is necessarily limited, but all of
the books ever written could not come close to painting a complete
picture of our complex Creator.

This is one of the most amazing aspects of the life of listening
prayer that we are cultivating. To know God is not a one-time experience. It takes a lifetime of listening for His voice to scratch the sur-
face of knowing Him intimately, of understanding something of His
mind and His heart. Oh, we can know a great deal *about* Him; we
can read what scholars have written over the course of many centuries, but we have the opportunity to know Him, as He reveals
Himself to us, in small revelations every day. The truest joy of life as

a follower of Christ is that *we come to know God* not via a one-time revelation, but through a lifetime of discovery.

"And this is eternal life," said Jesus, "that they may know You, the only true God, and Jesus Christ whom You have sent" (John 17:3 NKJV). Jesus was talking about His disciples, the ones to whom He had revealed aspects of the Father's character over the course of three and a half years of walking through life together. And yet, for their good, He was praying that they might continue to get to know the Father—that they might see the Father at work in new and fresh ways—that the Holy Spirit would continue to remind them of what they had learned while they walked with Him on earth.

The initial rush of euphoria during the romance stage of a couple's relationship doesn't constitute a deep understanding of each other's character traits, virtues, and vices. In a few weeks or months they may "fall in love," but they can't possibly know everything about each other. It takes years of tireless, patient, and sometimes painful effort for each to comprehend the motivations, joys, and sorrows of the other, for each to bear the other's burdens with unspoken understanding.

The same holds true for our relationship with the unfathomable God. We come to know Him only as we dive into the deep ocean of His living Word, which (although we may have read the same passage dozens of times) at each reading reveals new truths to our searching hearts. The difference, of course, is that God already knows us. Before we were formed, He knew everything about us. Listen to the psalmist's words, "You watched me as I was being formed in utter seclusion, as I was woven together in the dark of the womb. You saw me before I was born. Every day of my life was recorded in your book. Every moment was laid out before a single day had passed. How precious are your thoughts about me, O God!" (Psalm 139:15–17 NLT).

Amazing. The God who knows my weaknesses, my sins, the things that trigger anger in me, the countless ways I disappoint Him and fall short of His expectations—that same God offers me the unprecedented opportunity to know Him to the fullest human capacity.

How does God unveil the truth about Himself to us? The Holy Spirit plays the pivotal role in this action. Paul explained this mystery to the Corinthians:

> That is what the Scriptures mean when they say, "No eye has seen, no ear has heard, and no mind has imagined what God has prepared for those who love him." But we know these things because God has revealed them to us by his Spirit, and his Spirit searches out everything and shows us even God's deep secrets. No one can know what anyone else is really thinking except that person alone, and no one can know God's thoughts except God's own Spirit. And God has actually given us his Spirit (not the world's spirit) so we can know the wonderful things God has freely given us. (1 Corinthians 2:9–12 NLT)

As the Spirit unveils the mysteries of God to us, what will we learn about our Father? Let me answer that question with one example: When He revealed to John the Beloved what would happen at the close of this world's history books, He gave us a glimpse of scenes human eyes had not previously witnessed. One of these bits of insight into God's arena is a terrible awareness of the things that cause Him pain—the sin, injustice, and dark forces that are contrary to His character. But as we see these, we come to understand that He is truly almighty, or, in our terminology, without contenders. According to one commentary, "No matter how fierce and wicked Satan may be, he cannot defeat God. In God's time and in His way He will fulfill His promises and accomplish His sovereign purpose in history."[2] Knowing God as the ultimate victor is an empowering, awe-inspiring privilege. This is but one of the countless revelations the Spirit can make to us.

And so, our prayers should be replete with requests that God's Spirit would reveal an aspect of the triune God to us each day; this is truly a prayer that falls within the domain of God's best interests for us.

PERSONAL PRAYER STARTER

———————— ⌒♃⌒ ————————

Spirit of the living God,
 I beg You to reveal the Father to me. I want to know Him. I
want to begin to understand the things that are important to Him.
 Please meet me here, and reveal Him as . . .
 As I search the Scriptures today, show me what You want me
to know . . .

———————— ⌒♃⌒ ————————

NOTES

1. "Spiritus Sanctus," quoted in Ken Gire (comp. and ed.), *Between Heaven and Earth: Prayers and Reflections That Celebrate an Intimate God* (San Francisco: HarperSanFrancisco, 1997).

2. *Nelson's Illustrated Bible Dictionary,* electronic ed. (Nashville: Nelson, 1986), s.v. "Revelation of John."

ॐ

FOR HIS
USE ALONE

ॐ

Holy, holy, holy, though the darkness hide Thee,
Though the eye of sinful man Thy glory may not see;
Only Thou art holy; there is none beside Thee
Perfect in power, in love, and purity.
—REGINALD HEBER (LYRICS 1826), "HOLY, HOLY, HOLY."

*A*s Jesus prayed on, interceding to the Father for His beloved followers (and for those who would believe and come after), He asked that we would be *sanctified* (John 17:17). Similarly, when He taught His disciples to pray, He began by teaching them to address the Father with these words: "Hallowed be your name" (Matthew 6:9). Jesus used the same Greek word in both instances; one time we translate it *hallowed*, and the other time we translate it *sanctify*. Since neither *hallowed* nor *sanctify* is a word we use frequently in everyday language, we aren't likely to comprehend their full meaning or significance. In fact, we've probably prayed the word in the Lord's Prayer hundreds of times, so often that our eyes tend to glaze over and our minds go into neutral as we recite it by rote in the presence of a congregation of worshipers. Well, then, maybe it's time for us to approach that phrase with fresh eyes and minds ready to be enlightened.

The Greek word Jesus uses is *hagiazo,* which means "to make holy, purify or consecrate."[1] This New Testament concept is consistent with what we know of God's character from reading Old Testament accounts of believers who encountered God face to face. When Isaiah saw the Lord "seated on a throne, high and exalted" (Isaiah 6:1), he heard the six-winged seraphs calling out, "Holy, holy, holy is the Lord Almighty; the whole earth is full of his glory" (v. 3). This passage uses the Hebrew word *qadowsh.* The meaning is the same—set apart or holy.[2]

Evelyn Christiansen explained to an audience during a recent concert of prayer that the only attribute of God that was ever noted in Scripture in triplicate is His holiness. Holy, holy, holy. He is three-times holy—completely holy. The same phrase is attributed to six-winged heavenly beings in the book of Revelation. These beings never stop saying, "Holy, holy, holy is the Lord God Almighty, who was, and is, and is to come" (4:8).

In the Bible, things that were designated as holy were set apart for God's use alone. The utensils used in the temple were special; they could only be used in worshiping God. In fact, portions of the temple were designated as the Holy Place and the Holy of Holies, places of limited access. The place where God's presence hovered was designated the Holy of Holies. Admission to this holiest of all places was most severely limited. Only the high priest could enter this place. Only once a year after various ceremonial cleansings and sacrifices could he approach the holy place where the exalted God dwelt. It was a place filled with the dazzling presence of God. When the high priest entered this place, he did so with fear and trembling, because God's holiness would not allow him to live if he had not made every preparation according to God's specific prescription.

Nevertheless, God has revealed Himself to a few select believers down through the scriptural account. Moses encountered God in a burning bush, which he was invited to approach *sans* sandals, because this was, after all, holy ground. It was just an ordinary, run-of-the-mill bush, but it suddenly became special because God was there.

The first response of all Bible characters to the revealed presence of almighty God was to fall to their faces in humility and awe. Isaiah, God's prophet and chosen servant, fell to the ground wailing, "Woe to me! . . . I am ruined!" (6:5). In the pure and holy presence of God, Isaiah (even this good, upright prophet) gained a clear perspective on his "uncleanness."

What does this mean to us in our prayers?

First, it means that although God invites us to communicate with Him, we would do well to enter His presence with this proper perspective: God is holy, and the only holiness we can claim for our own is that offered to us by His Son, Jesus Christ. This is a difficult acknowledgment for us in our culture. We like to think we can clean ourselves up, make ourselves perfect, and be self-sufficient and complete apart from anyone else. But seeing God's holiness reminds me that only He is able to set me apart and make me worthy for His service.

And then, as I have been cleaned and prepared for His service, I need constantly to recall Jesus' statement that no one can serve two masters. I cannot be used in God's service one moment and then quickly change hands to be used in serving my own purposes or the Enemy's purposes. It is my responsibility to keep myself from being used for the wrong purposes, as God gives me the strength. This, then, is the prayer of my heart each moment and each day, that He might use me for His purposes and that I may be so occupied in His service that I am not tempted to be sullied by sin's filth.

PERSONAL PRAYER STARTER

Holy, holy, holy, Lord God Almighty,
   With the hymn writer, I recognize that though the darkness of this world may hide You from sight, though the sin in my life may blind me to Your glory, nevertheless, I acknowledge that You and only You are holy—perfect in power, in love and purity.
   Holy God, I ask for Your cleansing, that I may be used as Your vessel to . . .

I purpose to keep myself for Your service alone. So I set before You my tendency to . . .

Help me remain pure and ready to be useful to Your holy purposes.

NOTES

1. Strong's definition of Greek #37
2. Brown-Driver-Briggs' definition of Hebrew #6918

ᴄᴆ

UNITED CITIZENS
OF HEAVEN

ᴄᴆ

One hundred worshippers met together,
each one looking away to Christ, are in heart nearer to each other
than they could possibly be were they to become "unity" conscious
and turn their eyes away from God to strive for closer fellowship.

—A. W. TOZER[1]

We. They. Ours. Theirs. Collective words indicating that we are joined together in ownership or citizenship. When Jesus talked of His relationship with His Father, it was always "we." When He prayed for His followers, He consistently used the pronouns "them" and "they." He prayed for us as a unit—not by name, but interceded for as one package, related to one another by our common association with Him. A unit whose individuals would undergo the same kinds of trials and rejections by the world. A unit that, when working together, would have the potential to change the world; a unit that, when divided, would be a disgrace to its Master.

"That they may be one as we are one: I in them and you in me. May they be brought to complete unity" (John 17:22–23a).

One is indivisible by any positive whole number. And so it is with the indivisible Godhead—three in one—three individuals with different roles to accomplish the same ultimate purpose. Not quite comprehensible to the human mind, because there is none to whom we can liken this unique relationship. And yet, it is this oneness of purpose that we are to mirror to the world, as proof that He lives in us.

Is it one message that the world hears when we speak? Is it one heart of love for each other that the world sees when we interact among ourselves? Is it one mind that drives our passionate concern for the lost?

The sad answer to these is that if the world is to judge from the image we most often project, *unity* would not often be the first descriptor they would choose. Unity doesn't mean we must all follow the same liturgies, we must all sing the same songs (at the same speeds with the same instrumental accompaniments), we must all enjoy the same activities or agree on the best translation of the Scriptures. These petty disagreements divide us unnecessarily. The Bible was not written in King James English but in ancient Hebrew and Greek, which can be translated into modern English in a number of similar ways. Scripture does not prescribe a particular style of music for worship. God does not prefer high church to a laid-back, informal style, or vice versa.

Style isn't the issue with Him, at all. In fact, when the woman at the well tried to engage Jesus in a religious debate as to the appropriate place to worship God, He replied that regardless of the location, "the true worshipers will worship the Father in spirit and truth, for they are the kind of worshipers the Father seeks. God is spirit, and his worshipers must worship in spirit and in truth" (John 4:23–24).

So, if we don't need to be monochromatic in our stylistic preferences, what does Christ mean when He prays that we would be one even as He and the Father are one? The *American Heritage Dictionary* defines *unity* as "the state or quality of being in accord; harmony" and "singleness or constancy of purpose or action; continuity."

I particularly like the use of the word *harmony* to define unity. I am a violinist, having taken lessons since fourth grade. (Never mind how many years I have been playing!) I love the sound of the violin played well. Smooth. Mellow. Rich. Flowing. But other than practice times when I am learning new music or limbering up my fingers, I dislike playing alone. The sound of one is rather empty. Hollow. Without harmonic partnerships. Particularly skilled violinists can play short bursts of chords by pressing the bow into two or three strings at one time, but the fingerings are complicated and limit the capacity to skillfully play a melody up to tempo.

As lonely as one violin sounds by itself, that same violin when teamed with an accompanist or better yet an entire orchestra all playing from the same score (but not all playing the same notes) is a participant in something rich, something full, something alive. Melodies, harmonies, and countermelodies weave in and out. Sometimes the cellos take the lead, or the woodwinds, or the brass. Other times one violin's voice sings out in solo enriched by the accompaniment of the others.

If you've ever compared the musicians' scores, you know that only the conductor's score shows what every instrument will play throughout the piece. Line by line, this complete score lists each instrument's name and shows its note sequence, its rests, its holds, its complex patterns of sound. All of these are set in small print lining up vertically on each score page. Taken together, it is all rather dizzying.

Were the first violin section to attempt to play a piece while reading from the conductor's score, the sound would be muddied because the players' eyes would be distracted by extraneous notes. It is unnecessary for the first violins to see the notes the bassoons or the oboes or the violas will be playing. The first violins focus only on their notes; they let the conductor be concerned with the other sections.

This is unity. We in Christ's family are like the symphony orchestra. God is, of course, the Conductor and Keeper of the master score. Each of us has a part to play. We needn't worry about the parts others play. Each of us must focus on what God has called us to do—we must play our parts with precision and gusto.

Then, as each of us plays the part the Composer has orchestrated for her, the sound of unity will flow from us and touch the hearts of the world, so the world may know by our unity that we are in Christ and that He is in us.

PERSONAL PRAYER STARTER
———————— ✐ ————————

Master Conductor,

You know I have my own preferences, my own way of doing things. But I understand that were we all violins, each playing her own notes at her own tempo at her own discretion, the sound would be horrid.

Please show me only the notes You have arranged for me to play. I want to be a contributor to harmony, to unity in Your body, especially in the areas of . . .

I will keep my eyes on You and trust Your master conducting as I play my notes today, which include . . .

———————— ✐ ————————

NOTE

1. A. W. Tozer, *The Pursuit of God* (Camp Hill, Pa.: Christian Publications, 1948), 97.

CHAPTER 31

∽

AND THIS
IS LOVE

∽

What shall I say, O my God, my life, my holy joy?
What can any man say when he speaks of You? Silence offers the
greatest eloquence, yet woe to him who does not sing Your praise.

—AUGUSTINE[1]

*W*hen I took my entrance exams into graduate school, I had to focus a great deal of preparation time upon the English portion of the exam. (I was seeking admission into the journalism writing track, so my scores on the English portion were weighted heavily.) I still have nightmares about the questions on that intensive exam. Page after page was printed with comparison lists of complex words—some of which I had not previously encountered (and I consider myself to be fairly literate). The format of each question was the same: Word A is to Word B as Word C is to _____.

After hours of encountering these word relationships and extrapolating their meanings from root words, suffixes, and prefixes, my mind began to think in those parallelisms—looking for relationships between concepts that could be carried from one pair to the next. Not to deprive you of an experience with this brand of reasoning, I have a comparison question for you. As obedience is to listening, so is unity to _____?

Let's reason the solution out together. We established in chapter 26 that listening has to come before obeying. Obedience to God's law is impossible if we are ignorant of it, if we are too busy to hear His direction, if we have ears that are not attuned to the frequency of His voice.

Similarly, we cannot experience true unity without one fundamental building block. What is it? Let's look to Jesus' prayer for our answer: "May they be brought to complete unity to let the world know that you sent me and have loved them even as you have loved me" (John 17:23). Now we can answer the riddle: As obedience is to listening, unity is to <u>love</u>. Without loving hearts, we cannot exhibit a genuine unity within the faith. Conversely, love is clearly evident to all when our hearts are united.

In Matthew 22, Jesus emphasized the importance of love: "'Love the Lord your God with all your heart and with all your soul and with all your mind.' This is the first and greatest commandment. And the second is like it: 'Love your neighbor as yourself'" (vv. 37–39). Upon these, the greatest commands God has given us, hinge all other commands.

As He closes His spoken prayer, Jesus again mentions love. "I have made you known to them, and will continue to make you known in order that the love you have for me may be in them" (John 17:26). When the same love God has for His Son is in us, we can bask in the joy of lavish affection. But with the acceptance of that love comes a responsibility on our part. We must reciprocate it, direct it upward to God and outward to believers and nonbelievers.

The Old Testament term that described God's love was the Hebrew word *checed* (used 240 times, most often in the Psalms). It carries the implications of a lovingkindness expressed by the Creator through merciful dealings with the nation of Israel collectively and individually. *Checed* encompasses His generosity in providing for them, His strength in defending them, His longsuffering in forgiving them time after time.

How are we to respond to God's love, the love that while we were still held captive in the filth of our sin sent His only Son to buy us out of slavery?

We aren't to respond with a warm-fuzzy, romantically gushy feeling, but an active brand of love. Jesus said, "My command is this: Love each other as I have loved you. Greater love has no one than this, that one lay down his life for his friends" (John 15:12–13). So then, He expects from us an exhibit of God-love that is self-sacrificing, filled with generosity, loyalty, mercy, strength, and dedication.

This is one command God considers especially important, one that it is in our best interests to pray that we would display. Listen to this indictment of the church of Ephesus in Revelation 2:

> You have persevered and have endured hardships for my name, and have not grown weary. Yet I hold this against you: You have forsaken your first love. Remember the height from which you have fallen! Repent and do the things you did at first. If you do not repent, I will come to you and remove your lampstand from its place. (vv. 3–5)

They would be removed from God's presence if they did not renew their love for Him. A stringent consequence, it would seem.

In his first epistle John shows us why the consequences of lackluster love are so extreme: "Beloved, let us love one another, for love is of God; and everyone who loves is born of God and knows God. He who does not love does not know God, for God is love" (1 John 4:7–8 NKJV).

My computer has an indicator light that lets me know when its battery is fully charged, when it is ready to take on the task of being my silent partner in the writing process. If the light isn't shining, I must plug it into a wall socket to refresh its power supply. Likewise, love is the indicator light that tells God that we are charged up and ready to be useful to Him. It is the indicator to the world that we are His instruments, ready to bestow His love, His grace, His mercy to meet their greatest need.

Let's pray, then, that our indicator lights will shine brightly.

That our love for Him and for other people would be fresh and vibrant—like a bride's first love for her husband.

PERSONAL PRAYER STARTER

———————— ❦ ————————

Father God,

I love You. And I want to be one who shows Your love to a watching world. Today, I purpose to show my love for You by . . .

Likewise, I purpose to show my love for my family, my neighbor, my boss, my fellow driver, my friends, by . . .

Where I am lacking in love, please refresh and renew me from Your limitless supply.

———————— ❦ ————————

NOTE

1. Augustine, quoted in Ken Gire, comp. and ed., *Between Heaven and Earth: Prayers and Reflections That Celebrate an Intimate God* (San Francisco: Harper-SanFrancisco, 1997), 135.

ᴄᴘ

GLORY THAT SHINES THROUGH US

ᴄᴘ

Magnify to me Thy glory by being magnified in me,
and make me redolent of Thy fragrance.

—PURITAN PRAYER[1]

*O*ne of this world's favorite philosophies in these postmodern times is the premise that the human heart is basically good, that left to our own devices we will evolve to be better and better, that centuries from now our good natures will prevail and usher in an era marked by absolute peace, absence of crime, and eradication of poverty.

Wouldn't we, in our base humanity, love to believe this premise? But those who reason it out will quickly note the undermining fallacies. Given the choice between right and wrong, we humans have—from the beginning of time—consistently chosen the wrong over the right. We could shirk our responsibility and say with comedian Flip Wilson, "The devil made me do it." But the choice is ours, as it was with Adam and Eve in Eden. They *each* chose to bite into the forbidden fruit. No matter whom they blamed, ultimately the blame and the consequences belonged to *each* of them. We, too, must take responsibility for the choices we make; no one makes us choose wrong. We just do it. Naturally. As easily as breathing. It is what the Bible calls our sinful nature.

Let's take a passing glance over the devastation created by the evil in the human heart in our times. At Auschwitz. In Bosnia and Croatia. In the Middle East. And in the nightly news that hits closer to home. Shootings, gang warfare, bombings, robberies, and the like. Our friends and neighbors (surely not we ourselves?) seem to have patterned their moral lives after soap opera characters, living out in real life the fictitious filth they watch on their TV screens every afternoon. Even our leaders cheat and lie, proudly owning up to the sins of adultery and immorality, wearing scarlet A's on their chests as if they were badges of honor.

Do all these bespeak the innate goodness of mankind?

I'm sorry, but I don't see a world getting better and better. Sure, we have more technological toys every day—some call this advancement. But I don't see our culture advancing toward godliness of its own accord. Nor do I believe it can.

This is a debate that was ongoing even in the apostle Paul's day. I challenge you to read Romans 3 for Paul's list of the evils of which the human heart is capable. Let's look together at a key passage from that chapter: "As it is written: 'There is no one righteous, not even one; there is no one who understands, no one who seeks God. All have turned away, they have together become worthless; there is no one who does good, not even one'" (vv. 10–12).

So we humans, if we were left on our own, would be in a sad and worthless state for sure. Except we are not left alone. God has given believers a priceless gift, one that makes us stand out from the rest of culture. It marks us as His. It makes people jealous of us— either to the end of wanting to have what we have, or of hating and trying to destroy us because we have it. What is this lightning rod? It is the gift of God's glory. Listen to the proclamation of Jesus: "I have given them the glory that you gave me" (John 17:22a). We wear His glory, and like a brilliant evening gown it adorns us with more splendor than we deserve to have.

This is confirmed in 2 Corinthians 3:18, "And we, who with

unveiled faces all reflect the Lord's glory, are being transformed into his likeness with ever-increasing glory, which comes from the Lord, who is the Spirit." It is not in our own strength that we become more like God. However, through our relationship with God made possible by Jesus' blood, we receive power to become transformed into His image; so then the closer we get to Him, the more like Him we will look to those around us.

The *New Unger's Bible Dictionary* explains,

> In respect to man, [God's] glory is found in the things that reveal His honorable state and character, such as wisdom, righteousness, superiority to passion, or that outward magnificence that is expressive of what, in the lower sphere, bespeaks the high position of its possessor.[2]

In other words, God grants to us the opportunity to show His honorable character to a world sadly lacking in that necessary quality. He gives us a shine, a glow, an outward appearance that makes us recognizable as valued citizens of a higher realm. I don't pretend to understand how, but those who are walking closely with the Lord sometimes actually project a reflection of His glory on their faces. It's as though the heavy veil that separates humanity from God becomes momentarily transparent when a true believer passes by.

So there is a benefit to a watching world when we undertake a study like this one, when we seek more of God, when we expand the range of our communication with Him. For as we do this, we will reflect more and more of His glory, as a light that increases in brightness has the capacity to cut farther into the darkness. Let's thank our Lord for bestowing His glory upon us, and let's pray that He would continue to bestow it in increasing measure—not for our good, but rather for the good of a world otherwise blinded by sin's darkness, otherwise unable to catch even a momentary glimpse of the Father's glory.

PERSONAL PRAYER STARTER

Glorious Father,

What a privilege it is for me to receive the glory You have given to me. I know that in myself dwells nothing good, and yet because of Your sacrifice, I have the opportunity to reflect Your glory.

I ask that You would make me pure and clean so that my own sinful self does not get in the way of showing Your glory to the world. I especially ask this in the areas of . . .

And I pray for other believers, that they would continue to show Your glory in their spheres. I pray this especially for . . .

NOTES

1. "Spiritus Sanctus," quoted in Ken Gire, comp. and ed., *Between Heaven and Earth: Prayers and Reflections That Celebrate an Intimate God* (San Francisco: HarperSanFrancisco, 1997), 137.

2. *New Unger's Bible Dictionary,* electronic ed. (Chicago: Moody, 1988), s.v. "Glory."

CHAPTER 33

THE DRIVE
FOR PERFECTION

✑

*The best men in the world will readily own their imperfection
in the present state. We have not yet attained, are not already perfect;
there is still much wanting in all our duties, and graces, and comforts.
If Paul had not attained to perfection (who had reached
to so high a pitch of holiness), much less have we.*

—MATTHEW HENRY[1]

*A*s much as I dislike embarrassing party games, I very much like
board games that are won or lost on the skill and intellect of the
player. These challenges I find invigorating. My all-time favorite
board game is Scrabble™. Because of my reputation for winning (I
once beat a former boyfriend at the game; he sulked for days), I can
seldom find an opponent willing to take me on. Sometimes I play a
two-handed version, competing against myself or against the computer. Other times I make it doubly difficult on myself, not allowing any words with fewer than four letters.

I have put many hours of effort into perfecting my Scrabble
skill, because it is something I enjoy, something I find challenging,
something that increases my word mastery (a skill that transfers to
my work). Why, I wonder, am I more likely to put effort into perfecting my Scrabble prowess than to spend the same resources on

perfecting the spiritual skills that will lead me farther along the path of godliness?

My first answer is really a copout. *I can't be perfect in this life anyway, so why should I even bother trying?* This is partially true. I won't be perfect in this life. Neither will you. However, the Greek word Jesus uses to denote perfection is *teleioo.* It doesn't just mean the final accomplishment of perfection; rather, it encompasses the process of accomplishing perfection. It contains an aspect of moving toward the goal of blamelessness, of purity, of complete holiness. Listen to the phrase Jesus uses in John 17:23: "that they may be made perfect in one" (NKJV). *May be made perfect.* Not *are perfect.* Just that we can be one day if we are willing to make the sacrifices that will allow God to work the perfecting process in us.

In the meantime, perfection is a journey. As Paul told the Philippians, "Not that I have already obtained all this, or have already been made perfect, but I press on to take hold of that for which Christ Jesus took hold of me" (3:12). Perfection is a goal to be strained toward, deserving all the effort of pressing ourselves to the limit to attain, the prize that makes the strains and pains of the race worthwhile.

My second reason for shying away from seeking perfection is that I have an aversion to pain. Earlier Jesus told His followers, "I am the true vine and my Father is the gardener. He cuts off every branch in me that bears no fruit, while every branch that does bear fruit he trims clean so that it will be even more fruitful" (John 15:1–2). I am savvy enough to recognize that the pruning that will be necessary to make me perfect will cause pain.

Pruning. Maybe I *can* brace myself against that degree of pain. The lobbing off of unnecessary branches in my life, areas that are already dead or dying. OK. I'll make that calculated sacrifice. Maybe it'll turn out to be good for me in the long run.

But the Scriptures use another analogy for perfection that sounds much more painful. God, speaking through the prophets of the Old Testament, often likens the purification process to the extreme temperatures metalworkers use to separate gold or silver from the dross, the sludge, the gunk that contaminates it. "I will thoroughly purge away your dross and remove your impurities," God tells the Israelites (Isaiah 1:25). If you don't think this is a painful process, listen to a description from God's lips: "The bellows blow fiercely to burn away the lead with fire" (Jeremiah 6:29a). Willingly allowing God to perfect me through the refiner's fire is beyond me.

Then again, that may be intentional. Only God can steel my heart against that kind of pain. Only He can make me willing to step into that furnace. Perhaps Jesus' example will help me here. "Let us fix our eyes on Jesus, the author and perfecter of our faith, who for the joy set before him endured the cross, scorning its shame, and sat down at the right hand of the throne of God" (Hebrews 12:2). Talk about a fire. Only Jesus didn't need refining. As God, He has no flaws, no impurities, no contaminants. He endured only so *we* could be refined.

Watching Jesus interact with His Father through His prayer for us, I now know God better than I ever have before. The more I have studied, the more I have come to rely upon His proven judgments and His goodness in all His actions toward me. And so, I finally come to the point where I am able to say of myself what Paul said of the Philippians: "For I am confident of this very thing, that He who began a good work in you will perfect it until the day of Christ Jesus" (Philippians 1:6 NASB).

That doesn't make me look forward to the Refiner's fire or to the pruning of the Master Gardener. But it does make me willing to undergo the process of having my impurities removed, so I can move forward on the road toward perfection—confidently assured that I can trust the Refiner to protect me from destruction while I am in the flames, that I can trust the Gardener to remove only the dead wood. My prayer is that this study will have the same effect upon you.

PERSONAL PRAYER STARTER

———————— ✐ ————————

God, my refiner,
  I know my life contains impurities, dead branches. Make me willing to submit to Your pruning, to Your refining fires. This is difficult for me because . . .
  With Your help, I see the need for perfecting in these areas of my life . . .
  Help me, I pray, to press on toward the goal of complete perfection, which I know will come at last not in this life, but in eternity.

———————— ✐ ————————

NOTE

1. Matthew Henry, *Matthew Henry's Commentary on the Whole Bible* (Grand Rapids: Zondervan, 1961), "Philippians 3:9–14."

CHAPTER 34

❧

THE TRUE
CHRIST

❧

Unapproachable glory
Unattainable majesty
Inconceivable holiness
Hovered o'er the deep.
Spoke a Word and the world appeared
Separated the skies from seas,
Molded clay and the earth was filled
Breathed a breath — man came alive.
—JULIE-ALLYSON IERON & JOYCE IERON, "FILL THIS TEMPLE"[1]

I've been puzzling over the motivation behind Jesus' words in John 17:24: "Father, I want those you have given me to be with me where I am, and to see my glory, the glory you have given me because you loved me before the creation of the world." Why is it so important to Jesus that we would see the glory bestowed on Him by His Father?

We have discussed God's glory on several occasions. It is a theme that occurs frequently throughout Scripture. For glory is one of the attributes that contributes to an accurate picture of God. The true God. The One who is incomparable, indescribable, utterly incomprehensible to the human mind.

What do the angels of the New Testament say first as they present themselves, fresh from before God's throne, to humans? "Fear not!" The natural human inclination at seeing even a reflection of God's glory is fear and trembling. We instinctively know our place. That place is somewhat below glory.

Let's look in greater detail at what happened on one of the few occasions in Scripture when God made His glory partially visible to the imperfect human eye.

According to Exodus 33, "The Lord would speak to Moses face to face, as a man speaks with his friend" (v. 11). In the following chapter, we learn that Moses "was not aware that his face was radiant because he had spoken with the Lord. When Aaron and all the Israelites saw Moses, his face was radiant, and they were afraid to come near him" (34:29–30). He had to veil his face to address the people; they couldn't look on the reflection of God's glory that lingered with Moses whenever he had been with God. However, even Moses didn't see the full glory. God warned him, "You cannot see my face, for no one may see me and live" (Exodus 33:20).

Like His Father, Jesus too has an unapproachable glory. He chose to veil that glory when He lived among people as one of us. And yet, His glory remained. Remember what happened on the Mount of Transfiguration? Luke gives us a full account:

> As he was praying, the appearance of his face changed, and his clothes became as bright as a flash of lightning. Two men, Moses and Elijah, appeared in glorious splendor, talking with Jesus. They spoke about his departure, which he was about to bring to fulfillment at Jerusalem. Peter and his companions were very sleepy, but when they became fully awake, they saw his glory and the two men standing with him. (Luke 9:29–32)

Peter began to babble something about building some tents on the mountainside when suddenly the voice of God shook the mountain and the three disciples found themselves reduced to a trembling, bowed-down heap, as the Father audibly validated His Son's glory.

Such is the response of frail humanity to God's glory.

And yet, God has always wanted face-to-face communication with us. Sure He wants us to have a healthy fear of Him—an awed respect for His purity, His dignity, His ultimate superiority. But He created us for fellowship, for relationship with Him. In the Garden of Eden, before the man and woman sinned, God would walk with them, talking audibly, presenting Himself visibly. A division between God's realm and the human realm was unnecessary, because purity and holiness can face God without shame, without shadow, without guilt. The whole point of cleansing us from sin is that we will once again be able to stand in His presence—awed by His glory, but made holy and righteous by Christ's blood. The glory will no longer overwhelm us. It will envelop us. It will invite us to bow in worship. It will submerse us in the torrential flow of His love. But it will not destroy us in the burning fire of its awesome purity.

For now, we who are made righteous by Jesus' sacrifice can see that glory only with our spiritual eyes, but one day all that will change. We will see Jesus "coming in a cloud with power and great glory" (Luke 21:27). Jesus' prayer in John 17:24 at that moment will be answered, for we will with unveiled faces see His glory and live in our own glorified bodies (like those of Elijah and Moses on the mountain), remaining forever where He is. That is the moment to which Jesus looks forward, the thought of which kept Him nailed to a cross.

I believe it is important to Christ that we experience the totality of His glory, because He wants us to know Him as He truly is. He does not want to be hidden from us in any way. He desires that we see Him as more than buddy, more than even our sacrificial lamb, but as the Alpha and Omega, the Glorified Lord of the Universe.

All along, we've been looking for ways to voice prayers that are in the center of God's will. Prayers He will be pleased to answer. Prayers that are consistent with what we know to be true about Him. As we pray that we would soon see His flawless glory, perhaps some lyrics I wrote several years ago would be helpful. We began this chapter with a quote from the first verse of this song, "Fill This Temple." Let's conclude with the lyrics to the chorus, making them our heartfelt prayer:

Fill this temple with your magnificence

Fill the hollow in my heart with Your presence O Lord

Unworthy though I am

You have chosen to come in

Fill this temple, fill my heart

Creator Omnipotent.[2]

PERSONAL PRAYER STARTER

Glorious Master,

Again, I am awed by the glory that surrounds You. As much as I can in this life, I want to see Your glory with my spiritual eyes. And I pray that one day soon You will carry us all into Your presence, where we can bask in the glow of Your glory forever.

But I have many loved ones who don't yet know You. I want them to experience Your glorious presence for eternity. So, I ask You to make Yourself real to these whom I name here . . .

NOTES

1. "Fill This Temple," words by Julie-Allyson Ieron; music by Julie-Allyson and Joyce Ieron. ©1995 Julie-Allyson Ieron. All rights reserved.

2. Ibid.

PART FIVE

God's PROMISES TO US

Always and forever true to His Word,
our God promises us many gifts;
we, in turn, prayerfully can use
these gifts to further His kingdom.

℘

CHAPTER 35

THE SHEPHERD WHO IS ALWAYS WATCHFUL

℘

Frail children of dust, and feeble as frail,
In Thee do we trust, nor find Thee to fail;
Thy mercies how tender, how firm to the end,
Our Maker, Defender, Redeemer, and Friend.
—ROBERT GRANT (1779–1838), "O WORSHIP THE KING."

$\mathcal{T}$he more times I read and reread Jesus' high priestly prayer, the more I am impressed with the richness of truth about God that resides within these twenty-six short verses. This study, as much as it has focused on principles that will enliven our prayer lives, has become at least equally as much about the character of the God to whom we pray.

We have looked at His requirements of us as we prepare our hearts to address Him; we have sought out a biblically based picture of the almighty God; we have learned to carry to Him those things that are important to us; and we have learned to request of Him those things that He knows are in our best interest. Now we turn our attention to a technique of prayer that is even more tied to the Scriptures—namely, praying biblical promises back to God. Not to remind Him of these promises—He never forgets—but to assure ourselves that He cares for us, that He has pledged to carry our burdens, that once He has made a promise He will not fail to keep it.

Since childhood, I have recited the Twenty-third Psalm at least as often as I have recited the Lord's Prayer. In fact, as a small child I used to get them a little mixed up. "The Lord is my Shepherd, I shall not want. . . . He giveth me this day my daily bread." I was close. In fact, the picture of the Lord as a shepherd feeding his sheep faithfully day after day is rather accurate, theologically, even if I did skip a few thousand verses in my quotation. Jesus promised us, "I am the good shepherd; I know my sheep and my sheep know me—just as the Father knows me and I know the Father—and I lay down my life for the sheep" (John 10:14–15).

What does a shepherd provide for his sheep? Everything. He thinks for them—they are not astute enough even to find their way home without his direction. He keeps them fed and watered. He herds them gently onto the right path. He searches for those that wander off. He throws His own body between danger and the sheep.

In my years of following Him, God has proven Himself a careful and tireless Shepherd, fulfilling every aspect of a shepherd's role in my life. When I have faced frightening or difficult times, I have seen the Father answer Jesus' prayer in discernible ways: "Holy Father, protect them by the power of your name" (John 17:11b). I shouldn't be surprised at finding His goodness, His lovingkindness, His protective arm around me even as I "walk through the valley of the shadow of death." The God we serve, the God to whom we pray, has a character quality that we have yet to study—He is without exception *faithful*. Once He makes a promise, He will not go back on His word. Just look at His treatment of Israel. In Genesis and again in Exodus He made a covenant with them. Then, even though they continually failed to live up to their side of the agreement, He continued to live up to His promises. Paul explains to the young preacher Timothy, "If we are faithless, he will remain faithful, for he cannot disown himself" (2 Timothy 2:13). We are His sheep. He has claimed us for His own. And He has pledged to keep our souls safe until He can deliver us to our eternally joyful home in heaven.

Listen to verse 17 of Jesus' prayer: "Sanctify them by the truth; your word is truth." God's word isn't just a version of someone's perception of truth. It is *the* truth, the *whole* truth, and *nothing but* the truth. In fact, in Revelation, God assumes the name: Faithful and True (Revelation 19:11).

The implication of His faithfulness is that He can be trusted implicitly. But the requirement is that we must have an accurate understanding of the promises He made to us. Some people, unschooled in the reading of Scripture passages in context, careless about interpreting individual Scriptures in the context of what the whole of God's Word says about Him, build whole theologies out of misquoted or out-of-context interpretations. For example, Jesus never promised that we could demand anything we wanted of God. And yet some believers interpret Jesus' promise, "I tell you the truth, my Father will give you whatever you ask in my name" (John 16:23), as a name-it-and-claim-it promise that we will be rich, healthy, powerful, and influential in this world. In fact, what He did promise was, "In this world you will have trouble. But take heart! I have overcome the world" (v. 33).

Even Jesus, God as He was, did not demand His will over the Father's. When He prayed in the Garden of Gethsemane, Jesus didn't spout demands. He did make His desire known: "O My Father, if it is possible, let this cup pass from Me; nevertheless, not as I will, but as You will" (Matthew 26:39 NKJV). But He made no stipulations to His obedience. The tenderness in this request teaches us about the trust between God the Father and God the Son. The relationship can withstand honesty; and for both individuals, the greater good takes precedence over immediate pain.

So, as we personalize the Scriptures and the promises they contain to compose our prayers, let's remember not to take advantage of His faithfulness, not to presume a greater understanding of His purposes than we can have in our limited humanity, not to place ourselves on precarious ground by making demands of His graceful provision.

PERSONAL PRAYER STARTER

Faithful Father in heaven,

I thank You for being ever true to Your word. I am grateful that You will never change, will never go back on Your promises. So, with the psalmist, I ask You to be my Shepherd, that I may not be wanting in anything I need. I ask You to provide . . .

I ask that Your goodness and mercy would follow me today as I . . .

And I ask that You would one day deliver me safely into Your kingdom, where I will live in eternal sanctuary, face to face with You.

CHAPTER 36

ℒ✍

THE ABSENCE
OF INNER WARS

ℒ✍

"My peace I give unto you"—*It is a peace which comes from*
looking into His face and realizing His undisturbedness.
—OSWALD CHAMBERS[1]

ℒ‍ast Sunday afternoon our local PBS station aired a production of Franz Joseph Haydn's 1798 Oratorio "The Creation," featuring the London Philharmonic orchestra, chorus, and soloists. In the tradition of Handel's "Messiah," the instruments and voices of Haydn's "Creation" soared at the composition's apex (the creation of man and woman)—full and rich, uplifting and strong. Although this pinnacle was dramatic, I found the overture even more so. A male vocalist sang the Genesis 1 account: "And the earth was without form, and void; and darkness was upon the face of the deep" (v. 2a KJV). Ominous. Foreboding. Pregnant with anticipation. The accompaniment was solemn and muted, the vocal line written in a minor key.

And then, as light was separated from darkness, heaven from earth, land from sea, the oratorio increased in brightness and intensity. Just as God's peaceful order was established through each day of creation, the music followed suit, adding more voices and instruments in a controlled crescendo. The action unfolded as voices narrated each creation day's work, but every day the order remained intact.

Had Haydn's retelling of the story continued to the scene that occurred at the foot of the Tree of Knowledge of Good and Evil, I can imagine the sounds he would have composed to indicate the entry of the serpent, the first juicy bite of fruit drizzling down Eve's chin, the victory dance of the Enemy who succeeded in enticing the weak humans to disobey the Creator. My mind hears violins playing high-pitched helter-skelter scales—the first violin section dissonant from the second violins, trombones making slippery sliding sounds, each percussion instrument throbbing to its own tempo, a frowning conductor who appears to have lost control of the whole production.

And so it is with God's world. When the chaos of sin marred the picture of perfection, it tampered with God's established order. Like the conductor in our fictitious symphony, God allowed the sounds of chaos to be audible for a time, until the advent of the Savior. When Jesus died for our sins and conquered Satan by defeating death, once again order superceded chaos. The score called the instruments of our souls to realign with the melody.

Unfortunately, the externals haven't changed yet. The earth still shudders and shimmies, waiting for its redemption (Romans 8:18–21); many people continue to play their chaotic tunes. But for the believer, chaos no longer needs to pervade our symphony—it no longer oozes from the sounds we produce. God offers His people peace. This peace is not always outwardly audible, but it is the music that flows from hearts comforted, secure, and quiet.

Jesus acknowledged in His prayer the fact that the world's system would hate us, would war against us, would seek our destruction at every turn, would wish us anything but peace. "I have given them your word and the world has hated them, for they are not of the world any more than I am of the world" (John 17:14). It was not news to the Father that we are still living in the presence of our enemies; nevertheless, He promises to lead us like the gentle shepherd, inviting us to lie down in peace beside still and quiet waters (Psalm 23).

This world is full of hatred, of chaos, of decay and destruction. But the kingdom of God is full of love, of order, of glistening waters and shimmering golden streets. We come from a place of peace, so even when we live temporarily amid destruction, we take comfort that the "peace of God" guards our hearts and minds (Philippians 4:7).

Immediately prior to Jesus' breaking out into this magnificent prayer, He made this promise: "I have told you these things, so that in me you may have peace. In this world you will have trouble. But take heart! I have overcome the world" (John 16:33). Our source of peace, then, has overcome all the chaos, all the disorder, all the hatred and dissension in this world. He did this when He established peace between God and man, when He made a way for our cleansing from rebellion and sin. Listen to Paul's description of the unity Jesus accomplished between Jews and Gentiles, between people and God with His death and resurrection: "For he himself is our peace, who has made the two one and has destroyed the barrier, the dividing wall of hostility . . . to reconcile both of them to God through the cross, by which he put to death their hostility" (Ephesians 2:14, 16).

The promise we will use as we compose our prayer today comes from Jesus earlier in John: "I am leaving you with a gift—peace of mind and heart. And the peace I give isn't like the peace the world gives. So don't be troubled or afraid" (14:27 NLT). His peace isn't tenuous; it isn't fragile like the temporary détente the world negotiates for itself. His peace is permanent. All-encompassing. Liberating. It evokes inner security, trust in the control and power of the Master, freedom to go about the Father's business without worry or fear. And in the company of a generation that depends on artificial means to calm their minds enough to sleep, because of God's peace we can say with the psalmist, "I will lie down and sleep in peace, for you alone, O Lord, make me dwell in safety" (Psalm 4:8).

PERSONAL PRAYER STARTER

God of peace,

    I am eternally grateful for the peace of mind and heart You offer me. I want these—I want You to rule in my heart. So often I worry, fear, am disquieted. Please overrule these feelings in me by . . .

    Let me be an emissary for the kingdom of peace today as I . . .

    May I exude Your peace to help bring Your order to the chaotic hearts of those I meet today. And may my heart rest comforted by the assurance of Your peace.

NOTES

1. Oswald Chambers, *My Utmost for His Highest* (New York: Dodd Mead and Company, 1935), August 26.

∾

A PRIZE
WORTH PURSUING

∾

When my life-work is ended, and I cross the swelling tide,
When the bright and glorious morning I shall see,
I shall know my Redeemer when I reach the other side,
And His smile will be the first to welcome me.
—FANNY J. CROSBY (1820–1915), "MY SAVIOR FIRST OF ALL."

The next key promise of God that has a direct impact upon our prayer lives is the promise of eternal life. Jesus mentioned this both directly and indirectly in His prayer. "And this is eternal life," He prayed, "that they may know You, the only true God, and Jesus Christ whom You have sent" (John 17:3 NKJV). Then He reiterated, "Father, I desire that they also whom You gave Me may be with Me where I am" (John 17:24a NKJV).

The promise of our eternity with God is important to Him, and it can be a great motivator to us if we keep the promise before us every day. As the Scripture says,

Therefore we also, since we are surrounded by so great a cloud of wit-nesses, let us lay aside every weight, and the sin which so easily ensnares us, and let us run with endurance the race that is set before us, looking unto Jesus, the author and finisher of our faith, who for the joy that was set before Him endured the cross, despising the shame, and has sat down at the right hand of the throne of God. (Hebrews 12:1–2 NKJV)

I love the phrase "for the joy that was set before Him." He knew that ultimately His sacrifice would pay off in your salvation and mine. And that's what enabled Him to endure the shame, the agony, the unthinkable separation from the Father. Looking at Jesus' example, then, we can set before us the joy of eternal life with Him. This will make it easier for us to endure the sometimes painful race set before us: death's separation from loved ones, financial difficulties, illness and pain, disappointments and loneliness. Paul told Timothy, "If we endure, we will also reign with him" (2 Timothy 2:12a). The crown of life awaits us, if we brave the race to the end.

But if this promise is to be a true motivator, we need to understand a bit about what eternal life will look like. We've already established that in our human limitations we cannot begin to imagine an endless eternity where the tyrant time no longer regulates our lives. But the popular secular imagery of life after death is that we will be aimlessly floating around on puffy clouds, toting lyres and eating bonbons. Is *that* eternal life?

Surely not. Life is by definition vital, animated, active, and vigorous. Jesus promised us life abundant, life to the fullest (John 10:10). This promise begins its fulfillment in this realm, but it will not be fully realized until we step foot on the shores of eternity— where we will achieve the ultimate fulfillment and purpose through whatever activities God ordains for us.

Speaking of heaven's shores, to say the place He has prepared for us is beautiful is as much an understatement as trying to describe God as wonderful. John the Beloved described what he saw of God's holy city in Revelation 21. I'd challenge you to read that chapter in its entirety. But for now, suffice it to say the city "shone with the glory of God, and its brilliance was like that of a very precious jewel, like a jasper, clear as crystal" (Revelation 21:11). This is the city where we will live. We will have its name inscribed on us to identify us as citizens. Jesus promised this to those who would complete the race of earthly life, despite opposition: "He who overcomes . . . I will write on him the name of My God and the name of the city of My God, the New Jerusalem, which comes down out of heaven from My God. And I will write on him My new name" (Revelation 3:12 NKJV).

We do not have a complete picture of what we will do to occupy ourselves for eternity, but God will provide for us homes (John 14:2), beautiful garments (Revelation 7:9), jeweled crowns (Revelation 2:10), and feasts (Revelation 19:9). There we will have access to Him to worship Him, serve Him, and communicate with Him face to face. And throughout eternity we will bear His name, which He will have bestowed upon us with pride and joy—with great pomp and circumstance.

Whatever else eternity may hold for us, this incomplete picture is sufficient to be "the joy set before us," the incentive that will enable us to run to win this ultimate prize. And remember, "Eye has not seen, nor ear heard, nor have entered into the heart of man the things which God has prepared for those who love Him" (1 Corinthians 2:9 NKJV). The abundant and glorious life we will enjoy forever hasn't been visualized by even the most discerning human mind.

And so, in our communication with God today, let's not only thank Him for all the wonderful things He has planned for us in eternity, but let's ask that this knowledge will give us grace and endurance to face whatever comes our way in this temporal life.

PERSONAL PRAYER STARTER

Timeless and eternal God,

The glimpse You have given me of eternal life's glorious promise amazes me. May it motivate me to run with endurance the race I am engaged in these days, the race that . . .

Please keep eternity always close at hand, so that it may be the joy set before me as I face the trying times of . . .

How can I thank You enough for placing eternity in my heart? How can I find the words sufficient to let You know how honored I am that You have prepared such a marvelous place especially for me?

———————— ∽ ————————

ↂ

GIFTS
WORTH RECEIVING

ↂ

Breathe in me, Holy Spirit, that all my thoughts may be holy.
Act in me, Holy Spirit, that my work, too, may be holy.

—AUGUSTINE[1]

*C*arla and I were playmates when we were tots. Now she's getting married. Since she asked me to be in her bridal party, I'll be participating in several bridal showers. She and her fiancé have recorded their wish lists at various bridal registries. I enjoy combing shopping malls (now, there's an understatement!), and I've already begun shopping for the gifts I'm going to give at each shower. Some of these are on Carla's wish list. Some diverge from the list, instead expressing a bit of my personality and bespeaking our lifelong friendship. They are gifts that my years of knowing the bride tell me she will appreciate, even if she didn't know she wanted them.

That is, after all, the nature of gifts. They do not just please the recipient, but they also express the personality and the joyful spirit of the giver. It is as much fun to choose a gift for a loved one as it is to see her joy in receiving it.

God's gifts are no exception. James writes, "Every good and perfect gift is from above, coming down from the Father of the heavenly lights" (James 1:17). Jesus made a similar statement in His high priestly prayer: "Now they know that everything I have is a gift from you" (John 17:7 NLT). God the Son did not claim anything for His own. Every character trait, every ounce of power, every claim to authority, He attributed as a gift from God the Father. That's giving glory to whom it is due.

The gifts God gives to us are many. Salvation, of course, is the pinnacle of these. But He also gives us abundant life; enjoyment of beauty; love, joy, and peace. Sometimes He gives us items from our wish lists. Other times He gives gifts we didn't know we wanted. And some of His gifts come wrapped in the tissue of sorrow, pain, or disappointment. The child with Down's Syndrome who becomes a sweet blessing. The parent whose funeral celebrates a God-filled life. The loss of a job that challenges a believer to attend seminary.

Hear Jesus' words in His masterpiece of oratory, the Sermon on the Mount: "If you, then, though you are evil, know how to give good gifts to your children, how much more will your Father in heaven give good gifts to those who ask him!" (Matthew 7:11). God's gifts, like His character, are always good. They flow out of His loving heart. But they flow the most when we humble ourselves and ask of Him. Jesus invites His followers to "keep on asking, and you will be given what you ask for. Keep on looking, and you will find. Keep on knocking, and the door will be opened" (Matthew 7:7 NLT).

Not everyone receives the same gifts, or even an equal number of gifts (1 Corinthians 12:4). God designs each gift especially for the recipient. He who knows what is best for you and me bestows good gifts upon us willingly (not grudgingly). He hears our prayers, and ultimately *He* determines the gift He will bestow. But like siblings at Christmastime, we cannot measure our gifts against those He gives to others. "Daddy, you love him more because you gave him more stuff." That is unthinkable and childish.

Remember the biblical principle, "Everyone to whom much is given, from him much will be required" (Luke 12:48b NKJV). God's gifts are not purely for our own enjoyment. They come with a responsibility for us to use them for the benefit of His kingdom. Yes, they are signs of divine favor upon us. But they are also evidence of a trust—that if He gives the gifts, we will use them for His glory. Listen to Paul's explanation:

> We have different gifts, according to the grace given us. If a man's gift is prophesying, let him use it in proportion to his faith. If it is serving, let him serve; if it is teaching, let him teach; if it is encouraging, let him encourage; if it is contributing to the needs of others, let him give generously; if it is leadership, let him govern diligently; if it is showing mercy, let him do it cheerfully. (Romans 12:6–8)

We call these "gifts of the Spirit." These are talents and abilities with which God equips us. When we operate in His power, these gifts enable us to accomplish mighty tasks. Conversely, when we are detached from His power, these gifts will become as useless as clanging gongs (1 Corinthians 12–13).

When I was in college, I underwent a year of discipleship training at East Side Church of God in Anderson, Indiana. Our group of ten college students and two trainers met weekly, challenging one another to spend time in God's Word and prayer daily. One element of that training was a unit on spiritual gifts. We were to seek input from other believers as we identified our gifts from God. It is, after all, important for us to recognize our gifts and hone them to increase their usefulness. Our trainers were gifted in teaching. Others' lives exhibited mercy, encouragement, leadership, and more. Peter tells his readers, "Each one should use whatever gift he has received to serve others, faithfully administering God's grace in its various forms . . . so that in all things God may be praised through Jesus Christ" (1 Peter 4:10, 11b). And so, we learned to appreciate God's gifts and to use them productively in God's work.

Let's do the same today. Acknowledging that all these good gifts come from the Father's heart, let's pray that He would reveal His gifts in us, and that in using these we would be productive for His kingdom.

PERSONAL PRAYER STARTER

———————— ℘ ————————

Gracious Father,

Your gifts are as plentiful as they are good. I thank You today for the gifts of . . .

As I read Your Word, I see Your Spirit gives gifts to each believer for the benefit of the whole body. Please show me which gift or gifts You have for me, and confirm that through other believers.

Please equip me to use the gift of . . . that I may bring glory to You.

———————— ℘ ————————

NOTE

1. Augustine, quoted in Ken Gire, comp. and ed., *Between Heaven and Earth: Prayers and Reflections That Celebrate an Intimate God* (San Francisco: Harper-SanFrancisco, 1997), 140.

CHAPTER 39

ᴄᴘᴏ

AGENTS ON ASSIGNMENT

ᴄᴘᴏ

But drops of grief can ne'er repay
The debt of love I owe:
Here, Lord, I give my self away,
'Tis all that I can do.
—ISAAC WATTS (1674–1748), "AT THE CROSS."

*A*s I speak at writers' conferences across the nation, I am amazed at the number of conferees who write tirelessly every day with no assurance of publication. They write regardless of whether their words will be read by anyone. I am amazed at these folks, because they use their gifts in a different way than I use mine.

During my junior year in college, a professor convinced me the writing profession was a viable career option for me. Since then, I have been passionate about developing my craft. I can't say I love to write—I find the process somewhat draining. But I love *having written* because the printed word can touch hearts I could never touch. I am delighted to read correspondence from people I haven't met but who have been challenged by an article or a book I have written. I am thrilled when I am speaking at a women's retreat and someone tells me that my first book, *Names of Women of the Bible*, gave them new insight into the significant tasks God saved for women during Bible times. I will feel similarly about this book. These moments keep me recharged and able to continue writing.

Given an assignment, a deadline, and the knowledge that my words will reach a wide audience, I can be both efficient and effective. I will meet a deadline if it means sacrificing a social life, sleep, food, or exercise (especially exercise, which I find every opportunity to avoid). However, when the assignments slow to a trickle, I find other ways to occupy my time. Given a purpose, I will write for days or weeks on end. Without a deadline I cannot motivate myself to sit at my computer typing words that may never appear in print.

Purpose is a huge motivator for me. I am not alone. "Where there is no vision, the people perish" wrote the wise Solomon in Proverbs 29:18 (KJV). He recognized, after astute observation of human nature, that we must have a glimpse of the desired end if we are to be kept from sinking into the oblivion of boredom and purposelessness. Take, for example, the college students I teach to write each semester. Most of them are motivated to turn in their term papers and study for their exams not for the sake of the pursuit of knowledge or self-improvement, but only because of a single capital letter I will place in the registrar's permanent records after final exams. My students' goals are not noble, but they are motivators.

What, then, is our purpose in God's kingdom? What vision will inspire us to become productive agents in service of the King of kings? When Jesus prayed for us, He acknowledged to the Father that, although He was leaving the world, there was much work that yet needed to be done. He would complete His task between Calvary and the garden tomb. But that would be the beginning of the work He preordained for His followers. Listen to John 17:18: "As you sent me into the world, I have sent them into the world." Not to a friendly place. Not to a posh, comfortable life. He sends us to a world that misunderstands, hates, and tries to destroy us. Our mission—should we choose to accept it—is to become agents of the gospel who make disciples, despite opposition from the enemy and his henchmen.

Paul told the Ephesians, "For we are God's workmanship, created in Christ Jesus to do good works, which God prepared in advance for us to do" (Ephesians 2:10). Good works cannot earn us a place in God's family (Ephesians 2:8–9); nevertheless, the outgrowth of our love for God comes in lives budding with works that further the cause of Christ. Our purpose, then, is to find and complete the good works God has planned for us.

One of my most popular presentations to groups of all interests is a speech titled "I Can't Say 'No' & Other Time Management Myths." It is humorous and fun, but it packs a punch. It helps believers see that God had reasons for granting each moment in each of our lives. If we are to live with the object of entering Christ's joyful kingdom accompanied by the words "Well done, good and faithful servant" (Matthew 25:21), we must live each moment with His purposes in view.

As we each have different gifts, we each have different purposes. New Testament writers liken us to different parts of the same body. Each has a unique function. Each is imperative to the success of the whole.

As with the Israelites during their desert years, God will make His path plain to each individual who looks to Him. He doesn't leave us guessing about His purposes. Jesus promised that the Holy Spirit would "guide you into all truth" (John 16:13); God promised to make a path clear for those who trust Him (Proverbs 3:5–6). According to Isaiah, "The Lord will guide you always; he will satisfy your needs in a sun-scorched land and will strengthen your frame. You will be like a well-watered garden, like a spring whose waters never fail" (Isaiah 58:11).

Our prayer mission, then, is to look to God for guidance, to ask for direction at every juncture of the day—when we rise up, when we lie down, and at countless points in between. Our mission is to keep *His* mission ever before us.

PERSONAL PRAYER STARTER

My loving Master,

Thank You for giving my life purpose. I want to use each moment in a way that is pleasing to You, so help me to see Your plan—especially in . . .

Please equip me to pursue Your path with tenacity, even when I am tempted to . . .

Set before me today that portion of Your purpose You have planned for me to fulfill.

❧

CHOSEN
FOR CLEANSING

❧

Sanctify them by the truth;
your word is truth.

—JOHN 17:17

*S*anctification. A colossal label for a profound concept. It is deliberated in seminary classrooms. It is dissected by students of the original Greek. *Hagiazo* is the Greek word for "sanctify" that Jesus used in John 17:17. This rich word's variation of meanings includes the concept of purifying, of making clean; it also includes the idea of being separated from profane things to be dedicated for use wholly by God.

Jesus prayed that those whom God had chosen to be His followers would be made pure through the cleansing power of the truth. The process was this: First, God chose each of us to be His friends, His servants, His confidantes—He made this selection before the world's foundation was set in place. Then we sinned, bringing upon ourselves disqualification for service to a perfect and holy God. Next, Jesus entered human history, carrying with Him "the Way" to the Father; "the Truth" of the words that flow from the

Father's mouth; "the Life" that breathes immortality into those who were once spiritually dead (John 14:6). Finally, Jesus' prayer was answered in the affirmative when we made the choice to believe and obey the Truth we had come to know. When we took this step, the Spirit of God began the process of setting us apart, of making us clean and worthy of service to the holy God.

Let's look at that process more closely. Again, the Father chose us; we did not choose Him. Paul wrote,

> For he chose us in him before the creation of the world to be holy and blameless in his sight. In love he predestined us to be adopted as his sons through Jesus Christ, in accordance with his pleasure and will— to the praise of his glorious grace, which he has freely given us in the One he loves. (Ephesians 1:4–6)

He chose us so that He could make us clean and blameless, so that He could demonstrate His glorious and free-flowing grace through us.

In Old Testament times, sanctification was outward. Clothes were washed. Utensils and furnishings of God's tabernacle were anointed with oil. Holy people refrained from eating the meat of animals God called unclean or touching things designated unclean. Only then were the chosen few clean enough to enter God's presence.

Since Jesus came, sanctification has assumed its greater and eternal meaning: namely, that we be cleaned from the inside out, in a process we allow the Holy Spirit to undertake in our lives. Jesus told the picayunish Pharisees, "What goes into a man's mouth does not make him 'unclean,' but what comes out of his mouth, that is what makes him 'unclean'" (Matthew 15:11).

What are those things that come out of our mouths (and thus our hearts) that are unclean, that make us unworthy for service? Before he lists the fruit of the Spirit in Galatians 5, Paul lists the poisonous weeds of ungodliness: "The acts of the sinful nature are obvious," he says, "sexual immorality, impurity and debauchery; idolatry and witchcraft; hatred, discord, jealousy, fits of rage, selfish ambition, dissensions, factions and envy; drunkenness, orgies, and the like. I warn you, as I did before, that those who live like this will not inherit the kingdom of God" (Galatians 5:19–21).

These are the sins that would entrap every human being. But God . . . What an amazing truth! But God . . . made a way for us to be released from the trap. He heals the wounds the trap inflicted. He cleans us up and sets us loose in a grazing pasture that is trap-free. How gracious that He chose to save us. Hear 2 Thessalonians 2:13: "From the beginning God chose you to be saved through the sanctifying work of the Spirit and through belief in the truth."

So, even though several times in Scripture God challenges His people to "be holy, because I am holy" (Leviticus 11:44; Matthew 5:48; 1 Peter 1:15–16), He doesn't leave us to try to enact our own cleansing. How can anyone wallowing in filthy mud clean himself? Even provided with a clean towel, the one submerged in mud will watch helplessly as filth wins out over cleanliness. Likewise, we cannot make ourselves holy. That's why the "but God" is so amazing. God's Spirit accomplishes for us the cleansing we earnestly desire but cannot realize. It is our task to believe the truth of God's Word. It is the Holy Spirit's role to bring about our cleansing so we can be worthy of access to God: "For if you live according to the sinful nature, you will die; but if *by the Spirit* you put to death the misdeeds of the body, you will live" (Romans 8:13, italics added).

Our sanctification, our cleansing, is not a one-time deal. It is a lifelong process (Hebrews 10:14). God's Spirit continues to work in us to clean out the closets, the attics, the crawl spaces of our lives. He targets filth and clutter—great and small. For perfection cannot be accomplished, true holiness will not be complete, until every miniscule fiber of sin has been cleaned out of our lives. And so our prayer today will be that the Spirit would have full access to our lives, so that He will sift through and eliminate all of those hidden sins that are disqualifying us for the prize of holiness.

PERSONAL PRAYER STARTER

Most holy God,

I know that Your command is that I be holy, even as You are holy. I truly want to be clean. But I cannot accomplish this cleansing myself.

I thank You that because of Your Holy Spirit I don't have to clean myself up. So I give You complete access to the hidden spots of my life. Please reveal the dirt and cleanse me of . . .

I desire to live by Your Spirit, and to put to death these misdeeds . . .

Please continue this process of sanctifying me by Your truth until I am completely without blemish or spot.

∾

CHAPTER 41

WHAT'S IN A NAME

∾

His name shall be the Counselor,
The mighty Prince of Peace,
Of all earth's kingdoms Conqueror,
Whose reign shall never cease.

—WILLIAM H. CLARK (NINETEENTH CENTURY), "BLESSED BE THE NAME."

*W*hen I prepared to write *Names of Women of the Bible,* my research took me deep into the recesses of the Scriptures as I strove to understand the significance ancient Israelites placed upon one's name. This was a study I found fascinating, as I have always been intrigued by the meanings and derivations of words. I discovered that human names in the Scriptures often carry with them a prophetic element that looks forward to what that person one day will become. Eve, for example, means "lifegiver"; Ruth means "friendship"; Elizabeth means "oath of God"; Hannah and Anna mean "grace." Through the book's chapters, then, I was able to explore these meanings and their significance in the lives of those who bore the names.

Nowhere is the concept of the significance of names more pronounced than in the names God attributes to Himself. Do you recall the scene when God appeared to Moses in the bush that was burning but not consumed? The interchange is recorded in Exodus 3:13–14:

> Moses said to God, "Suppose I go to the Israelites and say to them, 'The God of your fathers has sent me to you,' and they ask me, 'What is his name?' Then what shall I tell them?"
>
> God said to Moses, "I am who I am. This is what you are to say to the Israelites: 'I AM has sent me to you.'"

God's name, YHWH (or Yahweh), was so sacred, so holy, that in Hebrew culture no human would speak it aloud. This is the name God told to Moses. According to *Vine's Expository Dictionary of Biblical Words,* the fact that God attributed to Himself the verb *to be* "is a declaration of divine control over all things."[1] Similarly, God proclaims the ultimate authority in His name at the close of the earth's history when in the book of Revelation He calls Himself "the Alpha and the Omega, the Beginning and the End" (21:6). He proclaims Himself preexistent to the beginning of time, and post-existent after time is obliterated. He always was, He is, and He always will be. All of that truth is packed into one little verb: "I AM."

The word used in the New Testament that we translate as *name (onoma)* "is used for everything which the name covers, everything the thought or feeling of which is aroused in the mind by mentioning, hearing, remembering the name; that is, for one's rank, authority, interests, pleasure, command, excellences, deeds, etc.," according to *Thayer's Greek Lexicon.*[2]

So His name is not only the label God wears or the manner in which we address Him, but it encompasses His character, His deeds, and most important His authority. When Jesus prayed, "Holy Father, protect them by the power of your name—the name you gave me" (John 17:11), and again, "I have declared to them Your name, and will declare it, that the love with which You loved Me may be in them, and I in them" (John 17:26 NKJV), He was calling upon the authority of that holy name to protect us as a demonstration of His power. Just as the name had been a source of strength to Jesus, it now can become a source of strength to His followers.

Bible commentator Matthew Henry elaborates on Jesus' request when he writes that the simple reference to God's name encompassed a rich array of requests:

> Keep them by thine own power in thine own hand; keep them thyself, undertake for them, let them be thine own immediate care. Keep them by those means of preservation which thou hast thyself appointed, and by which thou hast made thyself known. Keep them by thy word and ordinances; let thy name be their strong tower, thy tabernacle their pavilion.[3]

Here Matthew Henry alludes to Proverbs 18:10: "The name of the Lord is a strong tower; the righteous run to it and are safe."

I have this picture in my mind of myself running—panting, out of breath, fearful, lungs on fire, leg muscles rebelling each time my feet pound the pavement. Sweat-soaked eyes are barely able to make out the outline of the tower of God's name approaching on the horizon. Closer and closer it comes—but not quickly enough. Pant. Pound. Pain. Panic. Can I outrun the enemy? Desperate, with the pursuer closing in from behind, I call out the name of my Lord— and from the tower, He emerges. His arms are long enough and strong enough to grasp me, to pull me in to safety. The enemy has been defeated again, by the authority His name carries.

Such is the substance of the name of God that Jesus proclaimed to His followers. It is mighty and powerful. The mention of that name causes evil forces to flee in fear and trembling. It is a source of safety to the righteous, to the believer in Christ. And it is ours to use as we pray to the God who loves us, who protects us, who longs to bestow upon us spiritual blessings both in this life and the next.

We need no longer fear to speak His name aloud; in fact, He invites us to do so. Meditate with me, now, on this invitation from Romans 10:13: "Everyone who calls on the name of the Lord will be saved."

PERSONAL PRAYER STARTER

God almighty, great "I AM,"

    I am awed at the power of Your name. I am humbled that I have the privilege of addressing You by name.

    Since Your name is a strong tower of safety, I call upon that exalted name now to rescue me from . . .

    I thank You for keeping me safe in Your love even in this world where I daily encounter the threats of . . .

    Protect me, I pray, by the power of Your name.

NOTES

1. *Vine's Expository Dictionary,* elctronic ed. s.v. "to be": "Hayah".

2. *Online Bible Thayer's Greek Lexicon and Brown Driver & Briggs' Hebrew Lexicon* (Ontario: Woodside Bible Fellowship, 1993), s.v. "Onoma."

3. Matthew Henry, *Matthew Henry's Commentary on the Whole Bible* (Grand Rapids: Zondervan, 1961), "John 17:11–16."

CHAPTER 42

CALM DELIGHT

Fairest Lord Jesus, Ruler of all nature,
O Thou of God and man the Son,
Thee will I cherish, Thee will I honor,
Thou, my soul's glory, joy, and crown.
—"FAIREST LORD JESUS" (TRANSLATED FROM GERMAN TO ENGLISH
BY JOSEPH AUGUST SEISS, 1873)

In John 17:13 Jesus said to His Father, "I am coming to you now, but I say these things while I am still in the world, so that they may have the full measure of my joy within them." The phrase "the full measure of my joy" is the issue we will consider today. What is that joy, and why is it something Jesus prayed for us to have to the fullest measure?

According to *Strong's Greek and Hebrew Dictionary*, the Greek word for "joy" carries with it the implication of "calm delight." We in the twenty-first-century Western world are happy when all our needs are met and life is flowing along on smooth seas, but that isn't the full measure of joy Jesus meant. When an illness strikes or a loved one disappoints us or a rude driver cuts us off on the road, that happiness evaporates in a moment. Besides, no lasting gift from Jesus is tied to this temporal world.

Nelson's Illustrated Bible Dictionary explains that the Christian's joy is on a different plane than the counterfeit joy the world offers. Unlike happiness, joy flourishes even in difficulties because it is founded in the unchangeable character of God.

This is why the apostle Paul could write that even though he and his colleagues were experiencing gruesome suffering, their joy was full and boundless (Colossians 1:11–12; 2 Corinthians 7:4; 8:2). And that's why he could say, "We also rejoice in our sufferings, because we know that suffering produces perseverance; perseverance, character; and character, hope" (Romans 5:3–4). He was encouraging believers to find that inner wellspring of joy not *despite* circumstances but rather *in the midst of* circumstances. This is a subtle difference. Paul was encouraging us to look at sufferings as opportunities to develop the character traits of perseverance, character, and hope, which will multiply our eternal joy.

In answering the question of why our joy was a concern to Jesus during the last hours of His life, let's consider a phrase He used in describing the eternity of those who use their gifts and talents to further the gospel cause: "You were faithful over a few things, I will make you ruler over many things. Enter into the joy of your lord" (Matthew 25:21b NKJV). This is our invitation past heaven's gates: "Enter the joy of your Lord." So our citizenship in heaven includes eternal joy in God's presence. Listen to the way Isaiah 35:8–10 describes the picture in greater detail:

> And a highway will be there; it will be called the Way of Holiness. The unclean will not journey on it; it will be for those who walk in that Way; wicked fools will not go about on it. . . . But only the redeemed will walk there, and the ransomed of the Lord will return. They will enter Zion with singing; everlasting joy will crown their heads. Gladness and joy will overtake them, and sorrow and sighing will flee away.

Jesus wanted us to know that joy awaits us—unmeasured, unbelievable, otherworldly joy that cannot be dissolved by ugly circumstances earth-side. Like the joy of our salvation set before Him as He endured the cross, joy is the prize we see approaching, the promise of which keeps us motivated to complete the race.

But the joy Jesus offered wasn't just for some day, up there. Paul challenged the Philippians, "Rejoice in the Lord always. I will say it again: Rejoice!" (4:4). Always, every day, right here, right now we should have God's joy dwelling in our hearts, ruling our emotions, superintending our responses to difficulties, superceding our tendencies to tie contentment to circumstances. Joy is, after all, one of the fruits God's Spirit causes to ripen in our lives.

We may express that inner calmness and delight in God with exuberance or with prayers of gritty determination. But the joy that rests in the knowledge of God's goodness and love is unchanging. Psalm 71:23 resounds: "My lips will shout for joy when I sing praise to you—I, whom you have redeemed." In Psalm 42:11 the psalmist proclaims through clenched teeth, "Why are you downcast, O my soul? Why so disturbed within me? Put your hope in God, for I will yet praise him, my Savior and my God." Regardless, the joy God offers is beyond the capriciousness of emotions. It comes from God's Spirit, as Paul prayed for the Romans, "May the God of hope fill you with all joy and peace as you trust in him" (15:13).

When God gives gifts, He expects us to use them. Joy is no exception. "All joy" is His gift to us, one that makes us stand out as different from the world. As those who are serene. As those who are comforted in sorrow. As those who are contented with little or much. These differences will draw people in search of true joy to seek our Master.

Most especially, this joy must pervade our prayer lives. God cannot be pleased with prayers from a complaining, backbiting, discontented spirit. (Do you enjoy being around complaining people?) These are elements of our sinful natures that disqualify us from His presence. Instead, when our prayers overflow with joyful appreciation they become a fragrant aroma in His nostrils (Revelation 5:8).

PERSONAL PRAYER STARTER

My Master,

I find myself too often influenced by the rise and fall of emotions, baited into complaining and discontentment by the circumstances surrounding me. For this sin, I am sorry.

Please fill me, Holy Spirit, with the fruit of joy. I need this joy in . . .

Help me to focus on the joy set before me, even as I face the difficulties of . . .

Help me, I pray, to showcase Your joy, so others will see it and be drawn to You.

CHAPTER 43

HOLY, BUT NOT HOLIER THAN THOU

Rescue the perishing, care for the dying,
Snatch them in pity from sin and the grave;
Weep o'er the erring one, lift up the fallen,
Tell them of Jesus, the mighty to save.
—FANNY J. CROSBY (1820–1915), "RESCUE THE PERISHING"

I spent some time yesterday with a friend who has not yet become a believer in Christ. The last time we were together, I was planning a dream trip to Paris. So one of her first questions yesterday was about how I enjoyed Paris. I described the historic sights, charming bistros, and the best shopping spots on either side of the Seine. She wanted to know about Parisian men (I met none, other than bell-men, maître d's, and waiters) and the club scene in that hopping town. Since I had no titillating tidbits to tell, she quickly lost interest and moved on to another topic.

As a Christian, I am different from the world. My joy does not rise and fall with events and relationships in this world; it is founded in the bedrock principles of my faith: the unequivocal love of my heavenly Father, the successful completion of the tasks to which He has called me, the winning of new disciples to faith in Christ. Those differences make me almost unintelligible to people outside the faith. Those differences can also be useful tools of the Enemy to keep people from hearing the truth about Jesus Christ when I speak to them.

Take this scene that unfolds when I travel on business. I strap myself into the narrow aisle seat in the coach section of an airplane. Moments before the plane is to push back from the jetway, a harried traveler bustles down the aisle and gestures toward the seat beside me (the middle seat I had prayed would be empty). Once he is belted in, the requisite small talk begins. Having hoped for a quiet flight, I internally bemoan the fact that I can't bury my head in my computer screen because of the electronics ban on takeoff and landing. The conversation invariably goes like this:

"What do you do for a living?"

"I'm a writer."

"Oh, I've always wanted to be a writer. What do you write?"

Here's my problem. I write articles for Christian magazines; I write publicity materials for Christian organizations; I write books published by Christian publishing houses. You see the pattern here. I've found that, because of the well-publicized scandals among Christian leaders and the outspoken ways some Christians conduct themselves in public settings, the word *Christian* is a quick turnoff—it stops conversations faster than an emergency announcement from the cockpit. So I've taken to saying, "I write religious books and articles and do publicity for nonprofit organizations. And what do you do for a living?"

I want to be careful to qualify this. I am not ashamed of the gospel, and I do find ways to weave the message into conversation (usually about the time we begin our descent), but I try to do so in a way that won't shut the listener's ears before I have earned a hearing. I try to listen to the person in the seat beside me, to prayerfully consider how best to broach the topic of faith, to listen for God's direction in how best to "give the reason for the hope that [I] have" (1 Peter 3:15).

Yes, we Christians are set apart for God's service. Yes, we act in ways that are foreign to citizens of this world. We often speak a language they don't understand. In fact, these differences were a critical subject in Jesus' John 17 prayer/discourse. He reminded the Father that even as He (Christ) is from another realm, so are we.

But even as we cloister together into our family groups (a.k.a. churches), we cannot afford to forget that the service to which Jesus called us, the service for which our deepening prayer life prepares us, is to take place in this world, among its people—the very people whom we often turn off by our brashness, our condescension, our indecipherable conversation. "I don't ask You, Father, to take them out of the world," Jesus prayed, "but to keep them safe from the Evil One as they remain in the world, doing the work You have called them to do" (John 17:15, my paraphrase).

We must speak their language—within reason, of course. But we must learn to explain the gospel in terms from everyday life. Throwing around terms like *justification* and *sanctification* will do nothing to build bridges of understanding to those outside church walls. We insiders must place ourselves outside those walls, where the hurting people are. We cannot live our lives always and only surrounded by Christians. I find it enriching to build long-term relationships with small business owners who do not share my faith. Over time, I pray for opportunities to describe to them the joys of a personal relationship with Christ.

But, just as on an airplane, I must earn a hearing. I must show them I care about their lives, about their businesses, about the things that concern them. I must live out a faith that is relevant, uncompromising, and pure. If I preach, they will shut their ears. If I complain about the state of ungodliness in this world, they will label me a troublemaker. If I set myself up as a pious example of self-righteousness—showing them up for their unrighteousness—I will hinder the cause of Christ. If, instead, I show them a living example of the difference Christ can make in one life, perhaps they will be challenged to seek that experience for themselves.

Yes, we are set apart for God's service. But set apart is not the same as removal from the world. People we encounter every day are searching for joy, love, peace, understanding, forgiveness, acceptance—all gifts God bestows on His children. So, let's go ahead and be different because of our adoption into God's family, be guided by His Spirit, be conformed to the image of God's Son. But let's also work at interpreting the message of the gospel in a dialect the world will understand. Today, we will pray to that end.

PERSONAL PRAYER STARTER

Lord of the harvest,

You have set me apart, called me out of the world, so that I might be Your interpreter to a world that has a hard time understanding church language. Help me recognize those people You place in my life today who need You. People I meet as I . . .

In particular, I pray for _____, who doesn't yet know You. Please show me how to explain my faith in a way this person will understand. Soften his/her heart to make it receptive to Your message. Equip me to be a tool You can use.

CHAPTER 44

CHRIST IN ME, CHRIST IN YOU

*Most merciful Redeemer, Friend, and Brother, may we know you
more dearly, and follow you more nearly, day by day.*
—RICHARD OF CHICHESTER[1]

*O*ne way for a child to understand what it means to accept Christ
as Savior is to tell her Jesus will live in her heart. I can remember
when, as a tiny tot, I first told Jesus I was sorry for all the wrong
things I had done and I wanted Him to forgive me for them. I invited
Him into my heart with all the understanding my precocious three-
year-old mind could muster. I was sincere. I understood what I was
doing.

Even as a small child, knowing Jesus lived inside me, I tried not
to do anything that would displease Him. Whenever I disobeyed
my mother or got "mouthy" with her, she would say to me, "Go to
your room, and don't come out until you've told Jesus you're sorry."
This was a more life-changing punishment than any spanking or
any grounding. Because Jesus did live in my heart and He was displeased with what I had done, that knowledge crushed my tender
heart. I remember many occasions when I would kneel alone in the

corner between my high dresser and my poster bed to pray, "Jesus, I am sorry for this bad thing I did, and I don't want to do it again. But, just in case I do, well—I don't know if You can do this, but—would You forgive me for that, too? I am sorry—and I know I'll be sorry if I do it again. And I want to go to heaven to be with You."

All of that may seem simplistic to our intellectual adult minds, and yet there is much truth to the fact that once we have invited Jesus to be Lord of our lives, He does promise to come into our hearts (the seat of our emotions) by faith (Ephesians 3:17) and to live not just *with* but *in* us. Jesus concluded His high priestly prayer with the words "that I myself may be in them" (John 17:26b). The knowledge that Christ—the pure and holy Son of the pure and holy God—lives inside me, that He hears my thoughts, that He sees my actions, that He understands the true state of my inner life, ought to make the same difference to me as an adult that it did when I was a child. I need to maintain a clean inner household because of Christ's indwelling—withstanding temptation even in my thought life; keeping short accounts with God by confessing sin before it takes up permanent residence; calling into submission all thoughts, words, and actions that are inappropriate for one with a new nature purchased by Christ.

I am intrigued by the selflessness of the closing words of Jesus' prayer. On His way to the cross to die a humiliating, excruciating death, the climax of His concern was that I would come to know the Father. No wonder Charles Wesley penned the eighteenth-century hymn "And Can It Be." "Amazing love! How can it be/That Thou, my God, shouldst die for me?"

Every believer who considers the promise that God would come to live in us is equally amazed. Paul described it as "the glorious riches of this mystery, which is Christ in you, the hope of glory" (Colossians 1:27b). Listen to the enthusiasm in the words Paul used to describe Christ's residence inside us: glorious riches, mystery, hope, glory.

The God of the universe could make His dwelling anywhere. He could have chosen to live in the most elaborate temple, in a shimmering cathedral, in the skies among the starry hosts. If He were going to choose to live in humans, He ought to have chosen the wisest, the most beautiful, the most powerful, the most popular, the most perfect. Instead, He chose to live in me—a nobody with more flaws and imperfections than I can count. And, knowing all your flaws as well, He also chose to live in you (1 Corinthians 6:19). Paul told the Corinthians,

> God chose the foolish things of the world to shame the wise; God chose the weak things of the world to shame the strong. He chose the lowly things of this world and the despised things—and the things that are not—to nullify the things that are, so that no one may boast before him. It is because of him that you are in Christ Jesus, who has become for us wisdom from God—that is, our righteousness, holiness and redemption. (1 Corinthians 1:27–30)

The glorified Christ told the church of Laodicea that He was knocking on the doors of their hearts, asking for admission, promising a glorious meal together (Revelation 3:20). That meal can be a life of constant prayer and communion with Him. So as we approach prayer with grateful hearts, as we invite Christ anew to live in us, as we promise to live differently because our bodies are the temples in which the holy God dwells (2 Corinthians 6:16), let's meditate on this verse of Charles Wesley's "And Can It Be."

> *No condemnation now I dread;*
> *I am my Lord's and He is mine;*
> *Alive in Him, my living Head,*
> *And clothed in righteousness divine.*
>
> *Amazing love! How can it be*
> *That Thou, my God, shouldst die for me?*

PERSONAL PRAYER STARTER

Indwelling God,

 I am amazed and humbled that of all places You could have chosen to dwell, You chose to live inside me.

 I hear You knocking at the door of my heart, asking for entrance. Enthusiastically and willingly, I invite You in to dine with me.

 I feel unworthy of being the temple where Your Spirit lives. My sins and imperfections are like neon lights in my sight. Please make me worthy and cleanse me of . . .

 May my actions, my attitudes, my thoughts and my words be worthy of Your hearing.

NOTE

1. Richard of Chichester was an English bishop who lived from 1197–1253. Quoted in Ken Gire, comp. and ed., *Between Heaven and Earth: Prayers and Reflections That Celebrate an Intimate God* (San Francisco: HarperSanFrancisco, 1997).

PART SIX

Interests BEYOND OURSELVES

Now we will step out of our comfortable little worlds and learn to pray for those things that God desires for His universal church and for all citizens of the earth.

CHAPTER 45

ORDER
OVER CHAOS

For God is not a God of disorder
but of peace.
—1 CORINTHIANS 14:33

_To date we have dissected Jesus' high priestly prayer from many perspectives. We have looked at requests that are in God's interests, requests that are in our interests, and requests that stem from God's promises to us. Now we turn our attention to the external interests Jesus expressed in His prayer; namely, that His order would be reestablished in this world, that Scripture would be fulfilled, that the gospel would spread, that the world would recognize His love, and that His people would be unified. These prayers take us beyond the boundaries of our limited experiences. They focus our attention on issues at stake in the world at large.

Today, we look at the reestablishment of the harmony God originally intended. When He called creation into being, God fashioned order out of chaos. The earth was devoid of form, shapeless and chaotic before God called it to order. Plants and animals in the Garden of Eden He organized under the authority of the man and the woman. Every plant and tree produced fruit in due season; every animal coexisted with its contemporaries, fulfilling God's commands to be fruitful, multiply, and fill the earth. But when sin entered the Garden through the disobedience of the two humans, all nature took on an element of sin's chaos. The ground shuddered beneath their feet. All nature was different because of sin.

Despite creation's groaning under the burden of sin, God maintained a semblance of order. Order that holds the planets in place as they circle the sun. Order that maintains gravity on terra firma and keeps oxygen filling our atmosphere with breathable air. While the Enemy's chaos is at work, the superior power of God's orderly nature continues to bring day and night in their rotation, seasons in proper sequence, life and livelihood to one and all.

A pattern of God's order is discernible in the way Jesus formulated His high priestly prayer. According to Charles Ryrie, "The Lord prays for (1) His own glorification (vv. 1, 5), (2) believers' protection (v. 11), (3) believers' sanctification (v. 17), (4) the unity of believers (vv. 21–23), and (5) the ultimate glorification of believers (v. 24)."[1] These priorities mirror the progress of our study so far: God's interests first, our interests second, climaxing together in a God-established, glorious future.

Because He is not a God of disorder but of peace (1 Corinthians 14:33), God has a particular order for believers to maintain. He likens it to a body with many parts, each performing its function but operating together with the same goal. When Jesus addresses our unification with God and with each other, He says His order should be demonstrated this way: "That all of them may be one, Father, just as you are in me and I am in you. May they also be in us so that the world may believe that you have sent me" (John 17:21). The order, then, comes from our residence in Him and His residence in us. In the eternal order of the Trinity, God the Father takes precedence; God the Son receives glory from the Father; God the Holy Spirit funnels all glory back to the Father and the Son. Our organization as a body of believers in submission to the Trinity has the purpose of proving to a skeptical world the validity of the relationship between God and His redeemed ones.

In the Lord's Prayer Jesus taught us to request that God's kingdom would be established on this earth even as it already is in heaven. A primary element of the establishing of His kingdom is the reestablishment of His original order, the coming of a lasting peace. The prophet Isaiah described the day order would return to the earth:

> The wolf will live with the lamb, the leopard will lie down with the goat, the calf and the lion and the yearling together; and a little child will lead them. The cow will feed with the bear, their young will lie down together, and the lion will eat straw like the ox. The infant will play near the hole of the cobra, and the young child put his hand into the viper's nest. They will neither harm nor destroy on all my holy mountain, for the earth will be full of the knowledge of the Lord as the waters cover the sea. (Isaiah 11:6–9)

Nature is eagerly awaiting the day Isaiah describes. Only then will it be released from its birth pains, its bondage, its chaos (Romans 8:20–23). All of creation recognizes the authority of God and awaits the freedom His kingdom will bring—all of creation, that is, except the majority of mankind. Men and women are largely unaware, unwilling to acknowledge the Creator who takes an active interest in the hearts of people. They go about their lives, living as if they will never be called to account. Yet we who are believers know that in God's order, everyone will be called to account one day. And so, our prayer must be not only that God's kingdom would be reestablished on this earth, but that mankind in general, individual men and women in particular, would see in the order of the body of Christ the unmistakable proof of our words about Jesus Christ.

PERSONAL PRAYER STARTER

———————— ⌇ ————————

Master of created order,

Chaos surrounds me. Wars, natural disasters, hatred, jealousy,
and perverted evil seem to be controlling mankind. Yet I know You to
be a God of order.

Please add my prayer to those of other believers: May Your
kingdom be reestablished on this earth. May You be at work in
reordering the chaos taking place in . . .

May we, Your body of believers, be ordered and unified from
within, that we might show the world a pattern of the unity of Your
Trinity. In particular, I pray that . . .

Thank You for the peace Your order brings.

———————— ⌇ ————————

NOTE

1. *Ryrie Study Bible Expanded Edition,* NASB (Chicago: Moody, 1995), s.v. "John 17:1."

CHAPTER 46

∽

PRAYING
IN GOD'S WILL

∽

Enable me to do what is pleasing to thee;
give me that grace that is necessary to the right knowledge of thy will,
and an acceptable obedience to it.

—MATTHEW HENRY[1]

$\mathcal{W}$hen we embarked on this study, we determined to focus on the lessons of prayer we could glean from the intercessory prayer Jesus spoke for His disciples, recorded in John 17. That we have done. But, as we focus on prayer that takes us outside ourselves, we would be remiss if we didn't return momentarily to the Lord's Prayer. Consider the request, "Your kingdom come, your will be done on earth as it is in heaven" (Matthew 6:10). Jesus asked the disciples to pray into being God's will on earth. How is that possible?

God's will is a theme that recurs in Paul's letters, especially in Colossians, where he writes, "Since the day we heard about you, we have not stopped praying for you and asking God to fill you with the knowledge of his will through all spiritual wisdom and understanding" (1:9). Then he passes along greetings from Epaphras, who "is always wrestling in prayer for you, that you may stand firm in all the will of God, mature and fully assured" (4:12b). I love this picture of a godly person wrestling in prayer for fellow believers.

The apostle John contends that our prayers must be anchored in God's will: "This is the assurance we have in approaching God: that if we ask anything according to his will, he hears us. And if we know that he hears us—whatever we ask—we know that we have what we asked of him" (1 John 5:14–15). You'll recall that John was one of the disciples whom Jesus taught to pray. He heard the Master say that believers would have anything for which they asked the Father in Jesus' name. It is helpful, then, when John clarifies that "asking in Jesus' name" is another way of saying "asking according to God's will." Why does God not always answer our prayers in the way we wish He would? Because those prayers are either not according to His will or not in His will at the present time.

What do we know about God's will? One of the key elements of His will is found in 2 Peter 3:9, where we read of His compassionate heart, "The Lord . . . is longsuffering toward us, not willing that any should perish but that all should come to repentance" (NKJV). His loving heart breaks over all souls who choose wrong over right, who choose an eternity of doom by not acknowledging His claim of lordship over their lives. Jesus said, "For my Father's will is that everyone who looks to the Son and believes in him shall have eternal life, and I will raise him up at the last day" (John 6:40).

Another fact about God's will is that we can know it for ourselves. Remember, Paul and Epaphras prayed for the Colossians that they would come to know and understand God's will. Additionally, Paul advised the Romans, "Do not conform any longer to the pattern of this world, but be transformed by the renewing of your mind. Then you will be able to test and approve what God's will is—his good, pleasing and perfect will" (12:2). This passage stipulates that to know God's will, we must renew our minds by the power of God's Spirit. We cannot continue to think like sinful humans while expecting to think on God's plane. God's will is holy and pure. His ways, according to Isaiah 55:8–9, are higher than our ways and His thoughts higher than our thoughts. We must be purified—Paul calls it "having the mind of Christ" (see 1 Corinthians 2:16)—before we can tap into the knowledge of His will. Once we know and do His will, Jesus said we then will be called His brothers and sisters (Matthew 12:50).

When in the high priestly prayer Jesus directly addresses the topic of the fulfillment of God's will, it is in a rather negative context. He says: "None has been lost except the one doomed to destruction so that Scripture would be fulfilled" (John 17:12). The implication is that no one can stand in the way of God's purpose; Scripture will be fulfilled simply because it is the Word that proceeds from the mouth of God. This is consistent with the prophecy, "So is my word that goes out from my mouth: It will not return to me empty, but will accomplish what I desire and achieve the purpose for which I sent it" (Isaiah 55:11).

It is helpful to acknowledge that God's will does not always jibe with our wills. It was a struggle Jesus verbalized in the Garden of Gethsemane: "My Father, if it is possible, may this cup be taken from me. Yet not as I will, but as you will" (Matthew 26:39). Our lesson from Christ in praying the Father's will returns to a subject we studied earlier: submission. When we don't understand, when we don't like what God calls us to do, even then we need to submit our wills to His, acknowledging His authority to make choices that affect our lives.

Knowing all this about God's will, we approach today's prayer time. For ourselves, we pray that we would be willing to do whatever God wills for us to do. For other believers, we pray that they will know and stand firm in the will of God. For those who do not believe, we pray that their eyes will be enlightened to the privilege of being Christ's brothers and sisters.

PERSONAL PRAYER STARTER

———————— ℘ ————————

Heavenly Father,

May Your will be done on earth as it is in heaven. May Your will be done in my life. Please make me willing to do what I know You want me to do, especially . . .

For my fellow believers I pray that You would make Your will plain to them. I bring before You . . .

For those who do not know You (especially _____), I ask that You make Yourself plain to them, because I know You are not willing for any to enter eternal doom.

———————— ℘ ————————

NOTE

1. Matthew Henry, *Matthew Henry's Commentary on the Whole Bible* (Grand Rapids: Zondervan, 1961), "Matthew 6:9–15."

☙

CHAPTER 47

"IN IT"
NOT "OF IT"

☙

As you sent me into the world,
I have sent them into the world.

—JOHN 17:18

Think of the fork you use when barbecuing meat on your grill. It has two prongs, equal in size; both prongs and their long handle must be in balance if you are to turn the meat without singeing your arms. Similarly, our mission from Christ has two prongs. When we consider our mission, we are quick to quote from Jesus' final instructions: "Go and make disciples of all nations" (Matthew 28:19). Although this is an element of our mission, it is not in balance without its partner prong: prayer. Only when we have established clear, consistent communication between the Creator and ourselves are we attuned and equipped to address the witnessing prong—showing and telling people that Jesus Christ can make all the difference in the world to their lives. These two prongs of mission are attached to the handle—the foundational truth—that Christians do not belong to this world, but we are called to be at work in it. In it but not of it. It's a catch phrase—and a rallying cry.

Let's examine these two sides of the mission, trying to get a handle on where each takes place.

Until now we haven't addressed the "where" of prayer. I don't mean to debate the merits of kneeling versus standing versus sitting. Can we pray while driving? Yes! Can we pray while fixing dinner or sitting at our desks? Of course. The posture of our hearts before God is more important than the posture of our bodies, as Jesus told the woman at the well, "Yet a time is coming and has now come when the true worshipers will worship the Father in spirit and truth, for they are the kind of worshipers the Father seeks" (John 4:23).

As to the issue of where to pray (as a regular pattern), let's turn to Jesus' instructions: "And when you pray, you shall not be like the hypocrites. For they love to pray standing in the synagogues and on the corners of the streets, that they may be seen by men. . . . But you, when you pray, go into your room, and when you have shut your door, pray to your Father who is in the secret place; and your Father who sees in secret will reward you openly" (Matthew 6:5–6 NKJV). Jesus cuts to the heart of the matter: We must pray because we love and want to commune with our heavenly Father, not because we want everyone to know how spiritual we are. We are to pray privately (the King James Version says we should go into our closets), one on one with God.

Praying in public is not wrong. It is just not sufficient to develop a rich relationship with God. Public prayer is not the time for us to receive direction from God, to pour out our hearts, to "come clean" before Him. It is also not the time to preach at nonbelievers, trying to win them to the faith.

As Jesus continues His instructions on prayer in Matthew 6, He explains that the heathens (the pagans who worshiped idols) thought their gods would be impressed with elaborately worded prayers. The true God, however, is honored when we pray with genuineness, not trying to impress, but rather seeking a heart connection with Him.

As to the place of the second prong of our mission—reaching the lost—that cannot take place anywhere but in the world, in the public and private arena. That's why Jesus made the bold statement in His John 17 prayer, "As you sent me into the world, I have sent them into the world" (v. 18).

As I write, a debate is ongoing in Chicago regarding the plans of a Christian denomination to blitz the city with witnessing teams posted on strategic street corners. People outside the faith are incensed that Christians would target them. The denomination may be responding to God's direction received through prayer. However, from the perspective of unbelievers, a challenge to their beliefs (or lack of them) by a mass of strangers is unwelcome and distasteful. Let's think about their perspective. How would we feel if another religion—say the Muslims—were to target *us* for evangelism? They, too, believe they would be doing us a favor by converting us. But we would not willingly convert.

Only the softening of the Spirit of God can make a heart ready to receive the gospel. And that softening is often a result of our own intercessory prayers on unbelievers' behalf.

The message of the gospel is an offense—it is exclusive (Jesus said He is the *only* way to God), it is demanding (God calls us to be holy even as He is holy), it is formidable (the Christian life is like a marathon)—but we need not add our own offensiveness to that of the gospel. When we get the two prongs of mission out of balance—when we indiscriminately broadcast our faith without having first bathed our efforts in prayer—our attempts at evangelism are abrasive and offensive, and they may do the gospel more harm than good.

Although our mission is to take place in the world, without prayerful preparation alone in our closets before the Lord, without the empowering of the Holy Spirit upon our efforts, we cannot hope, as those *set apart from* the world, to have a fruitful ministry *in* the world.

PERSONAL PRAYER STARTER

——————— ⁒ ———————

My heavenly Father,

Sometimes I wish You would have taken us out of the world, rather than leaving us here to undertake Your work. It's hard to win converts to the faith. People act as if they don't understand my language. I don't know how to make them understand how important You are to me, how You have brought fulfillment and wholeness to my life.

I pray now for Your direction as I undertake Your mission to win the lost.

Show me whom to approach . . .

Teach me what to say . . .

Please soften the hearts of _____ that they may be ready to receive You.

——————— ⁒ ———————

CHAPTER 48

∽

A SIGN
TO THE WORLD

∽

*Almighty and tender Lord Jesus Christ, Just as I have asked You
to love my friends, so I ask the same for my enemies. . . .
I, a slave to sin, beg Your mercy on my fellow slaves.
Let them be reconciled with You, and through You reconciled to me.*
—ANSELM OF CANTERBURY[1]

𝒥 enjoy the notion that God loves me. I'm glad He loves you, too.
You're probably pretty lovable. We're family, after all—God's family.
I like to think that *we* are lovable, that He saw something in us, even
before we were cleaned up by the blood of Christ, that made us
worth loving. I like the fact that He loves *us*.

What I find unsettling, though, is that God loves outsiders. Sinners. Human beings who are His enemies. Citizens of this fallen
world. He loves people who torture His chosen ones, who are vile,
who are enemies of the church, who make life uncomfortable for
those of us in the faith. He loved the rulers of the Roman Empire
who fed believers to the lions. He loved the Pharisee Saul who
tramped about the countryside with the express purpose of killing as
many believers as he could seize.

And, much to our chagrin, He loves the people who work to
make our lives miserable—those who ridicule us for our faith, who

try to entice us to diverge from the straight road, who antagonize and frustrate our efforts. Doesn't it seem disloyal of Him to love *them?*

It depends on our perspective. If we look into the eyes of people who oppose God's kingdom, we will see something more unsettling: we will see what we would have been had it not been for God's grace. We, too, were once enemies of God. "But God demonstrates his own love for us in this: While we were still sinners, Christ died for us" (Romans 5:8). He didn't wait until there was something in us that made us worthy; He loved us while we were sinners.

"For God so loved the world that He gave His only begotten Son, that whoever believes in Him should not perish but have everlasting life. For God did not send His Son into the world to condemn the world, but that the world through Him might be saved" (John 3:16–17 NKJV). It's not to the pure that God gave His heart away, but to those who were filthy and in need of cleansing. It was to a world of people whose sin had earned them nothing but condemnation that He provided the free gift of salvation. It was to you and to me. "This is love: not that we loved God, but that he loved us and sent his Son as an atoning sacrifice for our sins" (1 John 4:10).

It isn't any old love that God holds for the lost. It isn't a warm feeling, a superficial pity, a passing fancy. Listen to verse 23 of Jesus' high priestly prayer: "May they be brought to complete unity to let the world know that you sent me and have loved them even as you have loved me." Yes, He loves His body of believers. But were it not for the fact that the Father loves the lost world, there would be no body of believers—there would be no blood sacrifice sufficient to wipe away our sin.

God loves the world with an everlasting love. An all-encompassing love. A self-sacrificing love. A love that gives itself away for its beloved. And He wants the world to know that He loves them.

God's love for His enemies is nowhere in greater evidence than when Christ was hanging from the cross. Love overshadowed His anguish and caused Him to relinquish the right to hold His crucifixion against His tormenters. Rather than demanding justice, Christ prayed lovingly, "Father, forgive them."

All of this affects how we think about—and pray for—the people who are enemies of the gospel. If we are to fulfill Jesus' desire for us, expressed in His high priestly prayer, we must be the flesh-and-blood evidence to our world that God loves them. To do this we must pray for grace and strength and courage. It is, after all, unnatural for us to love our enemies, to care for the eternal destinies of people with whom we would prefer not to spend eternity.

As our humanity struggles with this, let's listen to Jesus' command: "You have heard that it was said, 'Love your neighbor and hate your enemy.' But I tell you: Love your enemies and pray for those who persecute you, that you may be sons of your Father in heaven" (Matthew 5:43–45). His command is clear: Love *them,* and pray for *them.* Anyone can love lovable people. We must love the unlovable.

He makes this command, in part, because He knows our hearts will be changed in the process. We will come to love the lost as He loves them. But they will not necessarily come to love us. Author Eugene Peterson explains, "We must not imagine that loving and praying for our enemies in love is a strategy that will turn them into good friends. Love is the last thing that our enemies want from us and often acts as a goad to redoubled fury. . . . The enemies that Jesus loved and prayed for killed him."[2]

With the assurance that we will be made more like Christ and the hope that lost people might experience God's love, let's make it our habit to pray for those who oppose the church and the gospel.

PERSONAL PRAYER STARTER

Loving heavenly Father,
My first response is awe and gratitude that while I was Your enemy, fighting on the side of sin, You loved me enough to rescue me.
I understand, too, that You love those who are still enemies, who are still fighting on the wrong side of the battle. I think in particular about . . .

The individuals whom I just named need Your love and Your salvation. I bring them before You now and plead for their souls. Reveal Yourself to them. And, even though it will be difficult, I invite You to use me in the process . . .

NOTES

1. Anselm of Canterbury, 1033–1109, archbishop, scholar & writer. Quoted in Ken Gire, comp. and ed., *Between Heaven and Earth: Prayers and Reflections That Celebrate an Intimate God* (San Francisco: HarperSanFrancisco, 1997).

2. Eugene Peterson, quoted in *Between Heaven and Earth*, 105.

CHAPTER 49

ॐ

A UNIFIED FRONT LINE

ॐ

Dear Jesus, Help us to spread Your fragrance everywhere we go.
Flood our souls with Your Spirit and life. Penetrate and possess our
whole being so utterly that our lives may only be a radiance of Yours.

—MOTHER TERESA[1]

At two points in His prayer, Jesus prayed for our unity, so that we would present a united front in the battle for the world's souls. Twice in our study, then, we will visit this subject. You will recall that earlier we likened oneness to a well-disciplined symphony orchestra, where each of us focuses her attention on Christ our conductor and on the part He has written for her to play. This time, we will look to the Scriptures for direction on how we are to act toward our fellow believers, recalling that the impact of these actions has eternal consequences to a watching world.

What's the big deal about unity? We are soldiers in an army that is engaged in a battle for souls. Any division would weaken our testimony, make us vulnerable to enemy attacks. No army can survive the enemy's onslaught while it is wasting its energies and resources on internal sniping. Such "friendly fire" will bring down an army swiftly and decisively.

Conversely, our oneness, as each takes his place in the line, can bring a measure of security. It allows us to trust one another, to be more confident of victory even as we embark upon the battlefield that is of utmost concern to our loving Father—the battle to rescue spiritual prisoners out of the Enemy's camp.

Remember Jesus prayed, "May they be brought to complete unity to let the world know that you sent me and have loved them even as you have loved me" (John 17:23b). We can surmise, then, that unity is a sign to those outside the windows of the faith, those who are pressing their noses up against the glass, peering inside for any indication that God is alive and at work. We can show them that not only does God love us, but He loves them. But those who do not have the Spirit of God living in them can't see into the invisible world where God dwells. That's why Jesus didn't rapture us the moment we were saved. We are to show a picture of Him to the world—by our actions. They won't see God's love unless we give them an accurate picture through our love first for each other and then for them.

Having grown up in a Bible-preaching, fundamental, King-James-only church, how often I heard Psalm 133 quoted from pulpit and testimony pew. "Behold, how good and how pleasant it is for brethren to dwell together in unity! It is like the precious ointment upon the head" (vv. 1–2a KJV). But when I reread that passage this morning in a collection of modern translations, I gained a clearer picture of the benefits of unity. It is soothing, like a pleasant-smelling balm that soothes chapped skin. It is like the gooey gel exuded when you break open a stalk of the aloe plant. It brings healing; it eases pain. And so it is when we live with our Christian brothers and sisters (brethren and sistren?) in a unified heart. We not only soothe each other, but we show the world that their brokenness, their wounds, their sorrows can find healing in the hands of our loving Father.

I like the way the apostle Peter defines unity: "Finally, all of you, live in harmony with one another; be sympathetic, love as brothers, be compassionate and humble. Do not repay evil with evil or insult with insult, but with blessing, because to this you were called so that you may inherit a blessing" (1 Peter 3:8–9). Again, we get the picture of harmonious living. This time the harmony comes from the melodic tones of compassion, sympathy, and humility. It's a tall order that goes against the grain of my nature. He calls me to compassionate sensitivity with those who may sometimes rub me the wrong way. He calls me to sympathy with those who are suffering—whether their suffering is a result of unblemished living or a consequence of some sin. He calls me to humility, to treat others as more important than I. To place their interests ahead of mine. To carry them to God's throne when I feel I can barely limp there myself.

When God's love is operating, ruling, and reigning in our hearts, we *can* model this true inside-out unity to the world. Says the apostle Paul, "And over all these virtues put on love, which binds them all together in perfect unity" (Colossians 3:14). Having just told his readers to clothe themselves in "compassion, kindness, humility, gentleness and patience" (v. 12), the apostle shows that unity is the necessary outcome of this spiritual clothing.

Paul implores, "Make every effort to keep the unity of the Spirit through the bond of peace . . . so that the body of Christ may be built up until we all reach unity in the faith and in the knowledge of the Son of God and become mature" (Ephesians 4:3, 12–13). While he acknowledges that unity takes effort ("make every effort," he says), it is the desired outcome as we mature as a fellowship of believers. The "so that" reminds us that our unity will expand the impact of the body of Christ in the world.

And so, this is one of the major external interests for which Jesus petitioned the Father on our behalf: that as we grow up toward maturity in Him, we would grow laterally toward each other, presenting an army of Christ on the battlefield with no gaps, no splits, no sniping, no openings in the approaching line.

PERSONAL PRAYER STARTER

——————— ✑ ———————

Holy Trinity,

I pray for the whole body of believers, of which I am a part. May we learn what it means to be one as You are one. May we show Your love to the world through our unified front. I pray especially for my church, that we would be unified and that outsiders would know us by our love.

I ask that You would keep me from those actions that bring disunity. I fear that I sinned by promoting disunity when I . . . I ask Your forgiveness for those times.

I ask now that You would use me to help unify Your body by . . .

——————— ✑ ———————

NOTE

1. Prayer of Mother Teresa of Calcutta, quoted in Ken Gire, comp. and ed., *Between Heaven and Earth: Prayers and Reflections That Celebrate an Intimate God* (San Francisco: HarperSanFrancisco, 1997).

PART SEVEN

Postlude to PRAYER

The appropriate responses to all we have
heard Jesus pray on our behalf are
thankfulness, adoration, and praise.

~

CHAPTER 50

GATHER 'ROUND
TO GIVE THANKS

~

*Just as men spontaneously praise whatever they value,
so they spontaneously urge us to join them in praising it:
"Isn't she lovely? Wasn't it glorious? Don't you think that
magnificent?" The Psalmists in telling everyone to praise God are doing
what all men do when they speak of what they care about.*

—C. S. LEWIS[1]

$\mathcal{W}$e devote a day of every year to our next subject in prayer, but Jesus never directly mentions it in John 17. That subject? Thankfulness. In two of His other recorded prayers in the Gospels, Jesus begins with the words, "I thank You, my Father, that . . ." (see Luke 10:21; John 11:41). In truth, Jesus' thankfulness for the gifts of the Father is implied, if not overtly stated, throughout the high priestly prayer. His tone expresses gratitude to the Father for the gift of glory, the work assigned to Him, the provision of means to do the work, and the followers who would soon take on the mantle of fulfilling the work.

In the now-clichéd prayer acronym ACTS (adoration, confession, thanksgiving, supplication), a thankful heart takes the third place in the prescribed pattern of prayer. This may be, in part, because many times in the Epistles, prayer is coupled with the companion principle of a thankful heart. "In everything, by prayer and

petition, with thanksgiving, present your requests to God," Paul told
the Philippians (4:6). And when it came to advising his protégé,
Timothy, Paul said, "I urge, then, first of all, that requests, prayers,
intercession and thanksgiving be made for everyone" (1 Timothy
2:1). Similarly the psalmist wrote, "Let us come before him with
thanksgiving and extol him with music and song" (Psalm 95:2). Go
ahead and pray, but be sure to include thankfulness and appreciation
as you proceed.

As we opened this study, we focused our prayer on adoring God
for who He is. In thanksgiving, we focus our prayer on appreciating
Him for what He does for us. It is a subtle difference. Where worship leaves our needs out of the picture, thankfulness (sometimes
called praise) calls attention to God's mercy and kindness in His
dealings with us.

Apparently, thankfulness is yet another godly characteristic that
doesn't come naturally. I'd like to think if I had been one of the children of Israel traversing the wilderness behind a pillar of fire, I
would have been thankful for every time He provided manna from
heaven, for the fact that He saw that my shoes didn't wear out on
the journey, for every time He routed an enemy before my eyes. I'd
like to think so. But it is unlikely. Instead of thankfulness, God
received from the Israelites grumbling that the manna was too bland
in comparison to the aromatic spices of Egypt, unfaithfulness in
worshiping golden non-gods, and greediness in taking for themselves forbidden spoils from God's victories.

I think too of the ten lepers who begged Jesus for pity.

One of them, when he saw he was healed, came back, praising God in
a loud voice. He threw himself at Jesus' feet and thanked him—and he
was a Samaritan. Jesus asked, "Were not all ten cleansed? Where are
the other nine? Was no one found to return and give praise to God
except this foreigner?" (Luke 17:15–18)

Do you feel the grief in Jesus' words? Can you empathize with
the broken heart of the Healer—that His gift was received but not

acknowledged with thankfulness by nine of the ten lepers? Which leper would I have been?

We like to think we are independent, self-sufficient, in control of our lives. If we amass our own fortunes and maintain our own welfare, we have no one to thank but ourselves. But as believers in Christ, we have, by definition, acknowledged that Someone greater is in control. That Someone deserves our constant gratitude.

Earlier I mentioned the holiday of Thanksgiving, a day supposedly set aside to be thankful to God. In actuality (I'm not preaching to anyone if not myself here), it is a day when we women slave from the wee hours to stuff a bird, to dice and mash and bake and boil all the requisite fixings, while the family-room television blares the Macy's parade and a succession of football contests. I'm thankful, all right! Thanksgiving evening when it's all over I'm thankful this holiday comes only once a year.

When President Lincoln declared the last Thursday of November as Thanksgiving Day (to bolster morale during the Civil War), I'm certain this isn't what he had in mind. Throughout the history of the United States, days of prayerful thankfulness were declared by presidential order. In times of drought or emergency, they were declared for fasting and prayer. (Fasting, not overeating.) This is consistent with the biblical model of presenting our requests to God with thankful, expectant hearts. But today Thanksgiving is just another excuse for a day to take off work, to watch sports, to overeat, and to shop enticing holiday sales.

It's not that thanksgiving can only take place on Thanksgiving. Quite the contrary. Paul says, "In every thing give thanks" (1 Thessalonians 5:18 KJV). Not necessarily *for* everything—our hearts cannot be grateful for everything that happens *in* this life—but in every circumstance keep giving God thanks, keep doing what the old-time hymn writer suggests: Keep counting your blessings.

Prayer coupled with a thankful heart is pleasing to God. We come to Him, acknowledging our dependence on Him, asking for favors, and appreciating all the favors He already has bestowed on us. Let's be like the Samaritan leper, rather than the wandering

Israelites. Let's place thankfulness to God for what He has done in its proper order in our prayer lives.

PERSONAL PRAYER STARTER

——————— ✐ ———————

Gracious and giving Father,
    If I began to list all the gifts You have bestowed on me, I would need all of eternity to express my gratitude. But too often I grumble about the things I don't have rather than being thankful for what I do have. Please forgive me for this sin.
    I set aside time, today, to thank You especially for . . .
    Even as I ask that You would give me . . . so I thank You for every blessing You already have given.

——————— ✐ ———————

NOTE
1. C. S. Lewis, *Reflections on the Psalms* (San Diego: Harcourt Brace, 1958), 95.

CHAPTER 51

ℭℴ

STILL
INTERCEDING

ℭℴ

I have a Savior, He's pleading in glory,
A dear, loving Savior, tho' earth-friends be few;
And now He is watching in tenderness o'er me,
But oh, that my Savior were your Savior, too.
—SAMUEL O'MALLEY CLUFF (1837–1910), "I AM PRAYING FOR YOU."

I have looked forward to writing this chapter. Not because it means our study is nearing its end; not at all! Rather because the prayer principle we will study here is one of the most exciting privileges Jesus purchased for the believer. It's great that Jesus prayed one time for us, generically bunching us together as "all those who will believe"; but far greater is the promise we read in Romans 8: Both Jesus Christ and God's Holy Spirit continuously intercede for each of us, individually. Two members of the Holy Trinity live to intercede for you, for me. To whom do they speak when they make requests for us? They (and we) don't beg favor from an unfriendly, unfeeling, or disinterested judge but from the Father who loves us.

When Jesus took on human form, He limited Himself to time and space. He could appear in only one place at a time. He could only be with one group of followers at a time. But once He ascended to the Father and His glory was reinstated, He again assumed the characteristics of the Godhead, which include omniscience (all knowledge), omnipotence (all power), and omnipresence (presence in all places). So Jesus can be in me, here in suburban Chicagoland, at the same time that He is in you, no matter where in this universe you are. The Holy Spirit, too, has this inherent ability. Without omniscience and omnipresence Their continuous intercession for every believer could not take place.

Let's look at two passages in Romans 8 that enlighten us to this promise. First, we encounter the fact that the Holy Spirit gains God's ear on our behalf and mediates for us in words superior to ours, making requests that are more suited for us than anything we could ask for ourselves. "In the same way, the Spirit helps us in our weakness. We do not know what we ought to pray, but the Spirit himself intercedes for us with groans that words cannot express. And he who searches our hearts knows the mind of the Spirit, because the Spirit intercedes for the saints in accordance with God's will" (26–27). Marvin Vincent, in his study of words in the Epistles, writes that the Spirit "throws Himself into our case; takes part in it."[1] If we want to pray in God's will, we can trust God's Spirit to do that for us—as He groans with us, as He grieves for our trials, as He shares our pains, as He exposes our sins. I can't imagine a more loving picture than that of a God who searches our hearts—an intimate knowledge no human could share—then speaks on our behalf in emotive heavenly sounds that are superior to human language.

A few verses later, Paul says Jesus, too, intercedes for believers. "Who is he that condemns? Christ Jesus, who died—more than that, who was raised to life—is at the right hand of God and is also interceding for us" (Romans 8:34). The context adds a rich layer to the intercession. Because Jesus is strategically placed at God's right hand interceding for us, no one can charge us falsely before God, no one can place a wedge of separation between God and us. Jesus sees to that. When the accuser (Satan) wags his finger at me before God, Jesus tells the Father, "This one is covered by My blood. No one can condemn her; she belongs to Me." That's a fact even the accuser can't rebut.

In Hebrews, the writer pictures Jesus as the new and eternal High Priest who comes before God the Father to present petitions for His people. I love the phrase in Hebrews 7:25: "He always lives to intercede for them." Jesus *lives* to intercede for you and me. This is what He *always* does. Every moment He approaches the Father on our behalf. Marvin Vincent elaborates that Jesus "is eternally meeting us at every point and intervening in all our affairs for our benefit."[2]

Being a curious sort, I've wondered what the Spirit and Jesus say to the Father about me. The answer to that question is what this study has sought to uncover. What does God say to God; or, to put it another way, what do members of the Trinity say to each other? We have listened in on the communication between the Son and the Father as we have studied John 17. Another part of the answer can be found in something Jesus said to Peter on the night of the high priestly prayer. The disciples were in the Upper Room where they had shared the Passover meal. The eleven faithful men had pledged their allegiance to the Master. Then Christ said to Simon Peter, "Simon, Simon, Satan has asked to sift you as wheat. But I have prayed for you, Simon, that your faith may not fail" (Luke 22:31–32a). I tend to believe that Jesus continues to pray for us that despite all worldly temptations our faith may not fail.

For our own prayers, the end result of the fact of our two highly placed heavenly Intercessors is stated in Hebrews 4:16: "Let us then approach the throne of grace with confidence, so that we may receive mercy and find grace to help us in our time of need."

PERSONAL PRAYER STARTER

———— ⁀ ————

Holy Trinity,

Again I am awed at the value You place on me. That You, Father God, love me. That You, Jesus Christ, continue to pray that my faith will not fail. That You, Holy Spirit, groan before the Father on my behalf.

You know I am facing difficult situations, especially . . .

I don't know how to ask You to resolve these concerns. But You know. So, Holy Spirit, please search my heart; please make the right requests of the Father on my behalf . . .

I entrust myself to You.

———— ✑ ————

NOTES

1. Marvin R. Vincent, *Vincent's Word Studies Vol. 4: Epistles,* electronic ed. (Hiawatha, Ia.: Parsons Technology, Inc.), s.v. "Intercessions."

2. Ibid.

ALL
THE GLORY

Majestic sweetness sits enthroned
Upon the Saviour's brow;
His head with radiant glories crowned,
His lips with grace o'erflow.

—SAMUEL STENNETT (1727–95), "MAJESTIC SWEETNESS SITS ENTHRONED."

*A*lthough it is not in the earliest Bible manuscripts that have been unearthed in recent years, the traditional closing to the Lord's Prayer will give impetus to our wrap-up of this study. Whether it was added by a monk in later times or inadvertently dropped in certain manuscripts, this phrase serves as yet one more reminder of the awesome majesty of the One to whom we pray. If you are able, recite these words aloud as you read them. "For thine is the kingdom, and the power, and the glory, for ever. Amen" (Matthew 6:13 KJV). Let the words echo in the silence. Let their truth sink in. Read them again, as if for the first time.

Words similar to these resonate through the courts of heaven, where twenty-four elders constantly bow and offer this worship: "You are worthy, our Lord and God, to receive glory and honor and power, for you created all things, and by your will they were created and have their being" (Revelation 4:11). We've already established that the starting point to our prayers is properly awe and worship of the King of Glory. But I believe the pattern prayer we have used in corporate worship for years has something to teach us about closing our prayers by reiterating His majesty. "Thine is the . . . glory forever."

He doesn't need to hear us verbalize these words again as much as we need to speak them. After we've listed our requests—for those things in His interests, for those issues that affect our lives, for our loved ones, for spiritual growth, for unsaved souls, for a troubled world—it would be easy for our focus to remain fixed on the trials of life. It would be easy to come away from intense prayer downhearted at the plethora of painful circumstances in our fallen world. How much greater to leave the state of conscious prayer with a ringing reminder of the unparalleled power and authority of the One to whom we have entrusted our greatest burdens?

This phrase also gives us one more reminder of our ultimate goal of glorifying our Lord in every area of our lives. It is our task to bring Him glory on earth, even as He receives glory from the angels and elders in the heavenlies. When I conduct myself in a godly manner in public and private settings, I bring Him glory by enhancing His reputation. Conversely, my out-of-control conduct when I am frustrated, tired, or angry can bring disgrace to the Lord whose name I carry.

The fact that I am a reflection of His glory is a matter of constant prayer, so that I might be continuously transformed into His likeness—more loving, more kind, more gentle, more tenderhearted, more forgiving. Listen for one more description of Jesus, described by the Father through the prophet Isaiah and fulfilled by Jesus' earthly life:

> Here is my servant, whom I uphold, my chosen one in whom I delight; I will put my Spirit on him and he will bring justice to the nations. He will not shout or cry out, or raise his voice in the streets. A bruised reed he will not break, and a smoldering wick he will not snuff out. In faithfulness he will bring forth justice; he will not falter or be discouraged till he establishes justice on earth. In his law the islands will put their hope. (Isaiah 42:1–4)

This is a tender picture, a comforting picture of the Jesus who is ever interceding for us. When we are bruised—by our own sins or by the fallen world in which we live—He does not crush us; when we are trembling, He will not frighten us; when our candlewicks are smoldering and our light grows dim, He will not snuff us out. The Lord we worship does not condemn us, but He restores us, renews us, refreshes us, when we seek Him and when we carry our burdens to Him in prayer.

For these blessings, we bring Him praise. For His "radiant glory" and "majestic sweetness," we bring Him worship.

And so we conclude this study, returning full circle to where we began. Aware that every time we invoke Jesus' name in prayer, every time we address the heavenly Father with requests and petitions, we are entering a hallowed place, a holy throne room in the exclusive domain of the King of all kings. Now, let's enter that holiest of places together one more time—with grateful hearts for all we've come to know about Him, with worshipful hearts that have been made more tender by our face-to-face encounters with the mighty God, with petitioning hearts that He would continue to quicken within us those matters of prayer on which He knows we ought to focus.

Again and again, let us pray!

PERSONAL PRAYER STARTER

Majestic, holy God of my heart,

I feel as though I have seen You in a new light, as though I've met You on Your turf, as though I have heard You speak directly to me from Your own heart.

As I review all I've learned from Your Son's prayer for believers, these areas stand out in my mind . . .

I want this journey to have only just begun. I want to continue to know You as . . . I want to learn more about You. I want to meet You in all the comings and goings of my life . . .

And now, my whole being bows in awe of the grace, the majesty, the glory that surrounds You. "Amazing love. How can it be? That Thou my God shouldst die for me?"